ZEN AND THE HORSE

ZEN AND THE HORSE

---

*Body, Mind and Spiritual Unity
through the Art of Equitation*

Pamela J.G. Au

Library of Congress Number: 2002095815
ISBN :   Hardcover   1-4010-8190-8
     Softcover   1-4010-8189-4

This book is intended for entertainment purposes only. Any likeness or similarities to any work published or not is coincidental. There is no warranty or guarantee, expressed or implied concerning the contents or accuracy of this work. The author is not responsible for a coincidence.

This book was printed in the United States of America.

To order additional copies of this book, contact:
Xlibris Corporation
1-888-795-4274
www.Xlibris.com
Orders@Xlibris.com
17029

CONTENTS

PART FOUR
SPIRIT

To the horse,
. . . the greatest teacher of humility.

ACKNOWLEDGMENTS

My heartfelt gratitude goes out to all who participated in the growth and development of Zen horsemanship, whether directly or indirectly. There are many that participate on this level of understanding and stand alone in their efforts to bring to the world such an enlightened way of living. I acknowledge all spiritual warriors.

Special thanks to my loving husband, Jim; my two sons, Anthony and Joseph; Stuart and Jennifer Macagnone, Jan Ehrhorn, and my parents.

Author's photo by Krystina Scheller.

Illustrations contributed by my son, Anthony, Emerson Happy, and myself.

. . .

PART ONE
THE BASICS

. . .

INTRODUCTION

Nature is the force best equipped to provide and nurture the life it creates. Nature gives all animals the vital elements necessary for survival. As the paragon among animals, man is equipped with the same basic tools. Look at the miraculous design of the human body, it is capable of performing many tasks, and chief among these is the capacity to heal on all levels of existence. As part of its never-ending process, nature provides us with optimum equipment for the purpose of living.

There are countless physical possibilities and material limitations for every action. The law of balance in nature creates these limitations. Think of the flexibility of your fingers. Within their natural range of motion, they exhibit incredible strength and dexterity, yet are delicately structured and can only bend backwards so far before reaching the breaking point. If nature designed us so well, would nature have neglected the horse?

The way a horse walks, trots and canters are creations of nature. Every horse is endowed with individual range of physical motion, flexibility, and natural limitations based on their breed and habitat. Nature provides the rhythm and harmony of his gaits, and of your ability to perceive them. With your understanding of this natural rhythmic motion is the beginning of equestrian art.

The study of the horse's natural gait enables the rider's mind to record the rhythm of the horse. An experienced rider unconsciously translates this rhythm and applies it while riding. The horse is happy to work because he is comfortable traveling in his natural rhythm.

Alteration of the natural gait never produces brilliance, and it saddens the horse. Suppose you were asked to walk with your chin tucked and your back arched. Think of what this does to your natural gait and comfort. You would trade grace for the grotesque. The art of equitation demands preservation of the horse's natural gaits and spirit.

In general, humanity misunderstands natural law by placing emphasis on the manipulation and control of the horse. This develops disharmony in the rhythm of the horse and his partner. How can he move forward if his head is tied down or if the rider has a death grip on the reins? These are two of the many restriction that interfere with the forward movement of the horse. The outcome of these limitations is a man-made gait.

Nature has taught the horse how to go forward within each gait. We do not need to do this. Our responsibility is to teach the horse how to carry a rider in balance within his natural gait. To do this requires time and patience. For many, this is a challenge. Shortcuts are easier and faster, according to the logical mind. The human mind is the obstacle in the preservation and training of the natural horse. The need to change or control everything overpowers reasoning and humbleness. An individual must overcome his or her own weaknesses to become a master in the art of equitation.

The awareness of body movement, attitude of the mind, and their close relationship, allows us to master our physical, mental, and emotional conditioning thereby reforming our habits, which inhibits spiritual growth and harmony with the horse. This restructuring of physical, mental, and emotional habits releases the limitations of the mind and nurtures greater understanding of natural law.

The true art of equitation comprises three elements: awareness of body movement, attitude of mind, and unity of breath. Equestrian art, perhaps more than any other, is closely related to this process of restructuring the habits of body, mind, and spirit to allow a gradual unification of all three aspects of being.

This book presents a "way" of thinking, regardless of your involvement with horses. It is based on understanding natural law to enhance and preserve the natural movement of the horse. By doing so, personal growth is cultivated.

It is simplified into four stages: the basics, body, mind and spirit. Within each of these stages of personal growth are elements that comprise spiritual growth and personal success. These elements provide guideposts to develop your divine potential. This provides a nurturing environment for one of the noblest creatures on this earth, the horse.

. . .

WHAT IS THE ART OF EQUITATION?

Art is defined as a creative activity concerned with the expression of an idea. It is the concentrated efforts of the soul, an extension of the creator's work. Our purpose is to act as a conduit in which this creative activity can flow. This is accomplished through self-expression. It is a "way" of living that abides by natural law.

Books help to clarify and teach the concepts, techniques and mechanical skills of a given field, but they do not teach the essence of art. Acquired skills or techniques supply the foundation, but not the art. The essence of art is in your heart. It is something that you feel. It creates the standard by which you live. It is the "right way."

If an individual wanted to learn how to cut hair, the first step would be to learn the proper terminology from a book, and the mechanical skills from an instructor. This is simple. For haircutting to become a creative art means one must follow the guidelines of nature. The true art and design for the hair is determined by the bone structure of the face and head, texture and thickness of the hair, direction of hair growth, and body type of the individual.

Nature teaches the art of riding in this same way. Anyone can learn how to sit on a horse and make it gallop around. This requires a certain amount of skill, but it is not equestrian art. To learn the art of riding, the natural gait, rhythm and instincts of the horse must be observed and respected. Nature provides us with the proper hoof angles based on hoof quality and individual conformation of the horse. No two hooves are alike, nor is any horse identical to another. This individuality demands respect.

To ride a horse well, first, acquire enough skill and experience from an accomplished trainer. Next, practice, and practice some more to learn the natural rhythm and encourage clear communication. With concentrated effort, the wisdom of nature rewards you. It becomes second nature to look at a natural horse and determine how the horse should be ridden. Proper hoof angles are recognized and irregular strides are felt. The carriage of the horse indicates whether their rider has achieved a certain level of proficiency. This is nature's wisdom.

Equestrian art is the expression of a combined effort to produce harmony between the horse and rider. It is the ultimate goal. To reach this level of expression, the first step needed is a vision of the goal and secondly, the skill, talent, and devotion to achieve it. The physical and mental limitations of the horse must be recognized, as well as the limitations of the rider. Discover the talent of each horse and develop it, rather than force a horse with natural limitations to perform above their level of capabilities. Nature dictates the ability of each horse. Expound on that awareness. With this knowledge, the horse retains suppleness and purity of its gait. This ensures a good foundation for pursuing equestrian art.

With every art comes spiritual awareness and growth. A deeper understanding and reverence for nature is awakened. An insatiable yearning for the expansion of art dictates a way of life. An individual lives it through self-expression. Every thought becomes a catalyst for the development of art, training the body, mind and spirit. It is "the way."

A balanced rider/artist learns the rhythm of the horse by feel, sight, and sound, and then connects with this energy to create harmony and expression. This involves concentration, discipline and passion. The final presentation appears effortless.

Talent, skill, experience, and knowledge, combined with understanding, compassion and love for the horse, are the ingredients of an artist. The performance is brilliant, joining two kingdoms in an expression of harmony. This is true equestrian art.

. . .

THE ROLE OF THE HORSE

For hundreds of years man has utilized horses. They have been companion, laborer, and in current times, a trophy for the ego of man. Horses have evolved and adapted themselves to survive the ever-changing demands placed on them. They have been taken from their prairie lands and trained to fight battles, provide transportation, plow fields and compete amongst themselves. If given a choice, a horse would not pull a plow, carry a soldier or run races. Regardless, the horse continues to work for us.

Horses try their best to please us. Even under adverse conditions, they still try to understand and cooperate with us. This willingness naturally exists within the temperament of the horse. The social structure of the herd demands a certain amount of teamwork for the herd to survive. This innate willingness is transferred into our relationship with the horse. The affiliation is cooperative.

Riding a horse is an expansion of our athletic capabilities. It provides us with the opportunity to experience the same attributes as the horse has. The elegant frame and athletic build of the horse attract us, while its suppleness, speed and grace empower us.

Man's admiration for the horse dates back thousands of years to the first writings and petroglyphs describing the relationship. The virtues most recognized and admired then were courage, reliability, intelligence, and diligence. Today, these same qualities are still acknowledged and honored. These virtues added to the splendor of the horse, make it impossible to remain unmoved by the presence of a well-bred and well-trained horse. A thousand pounds of solid muscle, light in movement and distinctive in character, captivates an audience. The horse is obedient and submissive, forever raging with spirit. To us this represents freedom.

Those devoted to these magnificent animals never grow weary of the burdens they bring. Mucking stalls is a small price to pay when an animal of such magnitude greets you with a nicker.

One look into those large, fluid eyes, and the burden is quickly forgotten. There is no question as to the admiration and role of the horse.

. . .

CHARACTER

Every horse has a lesson to teach us. Some horses are explosive by nature, while others may be lazy or cautious, thinkers or daydreamers. By understanding the subtle differences, we can make adjustments in the application of proper riding and training techniques to aid in clearer communication and to avoid confrontations with the horse. With this experience, we become equipped with the tools to better understand different types of people in a variety of circumstances. This allows us to respond in a way that is conducive to the circumstance, instead of reacting without thought. Let's expound on that.

Suppose you own a six-year-old thoroughbred mare. She raced for a few years and then was sold to a beginner. After a year of frustration and injury, the beginner put her up for sale. She is a nervous but obedient horse with occasional mood swings. She is talented. You love her.

You take her out and groom her, only to find a new cut or scrape on her in the most unusual places. When you ride her, she trips over her own feet. Obviously, she is not traveling in balance. Improper training and handling, along with a lack of understanding, are contributing factors to the horse's lack of balance and insecurities.

If you pressure her, watch out, for she may explode with a temper tantrum. If it is one of her better days, she may give you impulsion that can unseat you. Her previous owners neglected her. This created in her a lack of trust for human companionship. What a challenge this type of horse is. In most cases, they end up going from one owner to the next, where they eventually meet their doom.

To make progress training this type of horse, first, trust needs to be reestablished. This is accomplished by building confidence. Patience, compassion, and proper schooling are essential to begin the re-schooling process. Confidence is gained by reestablishing her natural balance. She now is comfortable carrying the rider. Once the pain and discomfort is removed, there is no need for her to panic and run out of balance. The trainer replaces fear with confidence. Building confidence encourages her to trust in the rider or trainer. She now can perform within her level of ability.

The training of a horse must progress in a way that allows physical and mental development to be built upon the previous level of training. Each stage of training supports the next. You cannot expect a two-year-old to have the concentration, balance and skill of an eight-year-old, nor can you expect a horse in training level to execute a flying lead change or extended trot. These movements are too advanced for the level of mental and physical development.

To force or manipulate the horse before it is ready will make it lose confidence and trust in the rider or trainer. Most likely, this is reflected by a refusal to cooperate. The horse simply cannot do what is asked. At this point, the rider or trainer must be detached emotionally from the defiance in the horse. Simply ask again in a precise, calm manner. Communication must be implemented properly and clearly within the capability of the horse. By riding and training this way, the horse regains trust and confidence in its ability to perform and in its relationship with the rider.

In comparison, let us say you have a son with a similar personality. Maybe he is 8 years old. He is sensitive and his ego bruises easily. He has a strong need to express himself. He stutters when trying hard to communicate. He competes with his older brother, causing frustration. This develops into a lack of confidence. Minor cuts and bruises mysteriously appear on him. While playing ball, he trips over his own feet for lack of balance. He is a strong-willed individual.

Letting him surpass a small challenge within his level of ability establishes self-confidence. Developing self-confidence builds trust not only in one's self but also in the surrounding environment. The more trust established, the more confidence develops. Both attributes work hand in hand.

When discipline is required, a firm yet direct approach, without pressure, yields results. Mean what you say and follow through with the necessary actions. Discipline that is too lenient becomes an advantage, but applying forceful action will cause panic.

A frightened or insecure horse starts to run, fall on its forehand, change gait, or pick up speed to avoid confrontation. In the same way, an individual may lash out verbally, cower, become emotionally unstable, or shed tears due to insecurity. At this point, no learning takes place.

A horse's personality/temperament is as individual as a man's. We do not get along with some horses, while we are attracted to others. The same is true of people. There are those with whom we do not care to associate and others with whom we resonate. We can be frank with some people, while others may easily take offense. Some horses need firm discipline while others would feel hurt or rejected by strong discipline.

Occasionally, a rider's ego refuses to respect the subtle differences of personality. A mare that is in season, for example, may exhibit a resistance or stubbornness that may irritate or annoy the rider. Refusing to understand and look at the situation clearly, force is applied in efforts to manipulate the situation. Instead of complying, the horse rebels against any forceful action with superior intentions. This is nature's way. At this point, the frustrated rider feels powerless and loses control. The horse senses the rider's loss of power and most likely takes advantage of the situation. The result is an unproductive battle of wills.

A child who does not get his way immediately responds with a temper tantrum. The ego of man is like the child. He rebels against being powerless. He refuses to succumb to authority. The authority in this case is nature. Learn to be flexible and feel the subtle differences of personalities. Recognize the signs of powerlessness. Then, you will know "right action."

Right action is critical, whether it be riding horses or being in a heated discussion with your spouse. This skill is a foundation for developing harmonious relationships and bonding with your horse. From this foundation, it becomes easier to understand and abide by natural law.

. . .

COMMUNICATION

Nature provides us with different levels of communication. Speaking, tone of voice, body movement, feelings and emotions, facial and body expressions, and writing are examples of the types of communication available to us. Understanding all forms of communication is an important requirement in becoming a proficient rider and trainer.

For the rider, most of the communication is by feel. Subtle messages unconsciously communicate to the rider the needs of the horse. The cognizant rider immediately responds with the "right action."

Horses also respond to different levels of communication. Our tone of voice, the expression of our body carriage, and the way we walk send a message to the horse. Our mood or intentions are first communicated by the way we greet the horse. In the moment that the horse sees you approaching, his eye observes your gait and posture, his ear listens to the tone of your voice, and his mind interprets every body position or movement. The response is immediate.

This subtle form of communication happens on a subconscious level of understanding and is received and interpreted on a daily basis during interaction with others. This level of communication can be called *automatic acuity.*

Every day, we exercise automatic acuity, which means we unconsciously receive and translate information through the right hemisphere of our brain. The right brain does not receive or comprehend data through words. Instead, it processes information by looking at the entire picture or event, while translating the subconscious feeling of the picture, in its entirety, to the left brain, which then converts it to words, gaining understanding. The information from the right brain is perceived and communicated through the "feel sense" *(Part Four, Inner Rhythm)*, as a collective process incorporating all senses including the emotions. Activating the right brain through sight, sound and feel enables another means of communication and education. A good example of this is the sound of the rhythm in each gait of a well-balanced horse. A rider unconsciously learns to listen to the sound of each stride. This assists with the development of the feel sense, enabling the rider to determine the purity of the gaits and the natural rhythm of the horse. The sound is unconsciously translated into the whole picture and the rider uses this as a guideline to develop the right feel while riding.

Another form of automatic acuity is body language. Unconsciously, we perceive the thoughts and intentions of another person or of an animal by their body carriage and body alignment. For example: an individual, during an episode of rage or anger, approaches us with chest puffed out, fists clenched, and held breath, while a frightened horse may tremble, snort, raise its head and lock its neck, prick its ears upright, stand square and tall, raise its tail, and stand on its toes in preparation to bolting. The body posture of this horse communicates fear. Any observer can recognize this. These examples are the more obvious ones. The alert individual translates the subtle forms of communication and acts accordingly for the benefit of all.

The body carriage suggests to us the basic character of a person or horse. For example: A person who lowers his head and eyes while collapsing the shoulders when spoken to reflects a weak character or a low self-esteem. It is difficult for this type of individual to stand up for himself in confrontations. A horse that drops its head when approached indicates submission. This type of horse is most likely docile and willing to work for its owner.

Subtle communication is nature's way of talking. Riding provides the perfect opportunity to practice and understand these subtle messages. First, a conscious interpretation of the horse takes place, and then the right brain searches its library of feelings and instincts to interpret these messages.

Let's suppose you are riding down the long side of the arena on the rail. A sudden dust storm kicks up and the wind blows an empty feedbag against the fence at the exact moment you approach that area of the arena. Seconds before the horse spooks, you start to feel what the horse is about to do by its apprehension and loss of attention. At that instant, your eyes, ears, and feel sense automatically perceived and calculated the entire incident. A dangerous situation becomes avoidable or controllable as a result of this subtle form of communication.

Automatic acuity develops into what martial artists call *zanchin*. It is an applied awareness and alertness to the surrounding environment. This is not a passive state of mind; it is a dynamic state of readiness that implies instantaneous and appropriate response to a situation or circumstance. *Zanchin*, as a sense of perception, is more easily identified with intuition. For example: the ability to sense the intention of the horse before the horse has an opportunity to apply his intention. .

Animals maintain this state of heightened awareness, particularly those in the wild. It is *zanchin* that alerts them of the awaiting predator. This is sometimes referred to as "survival instinct." It is a natural response to the environment. A more subtle example may be that uneasy feeling you have when you decide to speed through the intersection to avoid the red light. On the other side was a police officer, waiting for you.

This dynamic state of readiness is crucial to the rider. It is the rider's only way of communicating and interpreting the intentions of the horse. *Zanchin* alerts the rider immediately, allowing effective communication and corrective actions.

In this heightened state of awareness, connectivity with the surrounding environment is enforced. There is a sense of oneness. Warnings and other subtle messages are easily communicated. Safety and a sense of control with the horse and the surrounding environment are supported as long as the horse has confidence in his rider.

The horse entrusts his safety to the rider. The rider can therefore sense and predict the actions of the horse before the horse has an opportunity to react. All forms of communication are active and alive. The rider's reflexes are quick and the brain engages without a moment of doubt. In a matter of seconds, the rider applies the right command and the horse responds.

This is called preventive riding. *Zanchin* allows the rider to prevent many dangerous situations by simply thinking like a horse. If the rider understands the nature of the horse and its response to certain stimulus, communication becomes clear and precise.

In order to achieve this level of heightened awareness, the rider first begins with a good foundation in classical horsemanship. From there, it is taken into a deeper level of consciousness. The right brain records all the actions and movements of the horse as the rider studies the horse in motion and learns through feel the proper rhythm within each stride while mounted.

Each time a rider strives to repeat a movement, the feel sense is activated. This helps the rider to find the rhythm of the horse and go with the movement instead of hinder it. Riding in this ways alerts the rider to any sudden change in the gait or abnormal movement of the horse. The brain tells the body something does not feel right and the rider responds by adjusting the body. The response is automatic according the rider's level of ability.

Beginners have not yet developed their library of "feel." Because of this, situations arise where they lack the awareness to sense and read what the horse is communicating. Thus, they are unable to execute the "right action". The horse responds by taking advantage of the rider.

Communication is an important tool for the rider. How else can the rider express his wishes to the horse, and vice versa? A constant level of communicating through the feel sense, *(Part Four, Inner Rhythm)*, listening to the rhythm in the gaits, and unconsciously perceiving nature's warnings are the determining factors for a safe interaction with the horse. Harmony and a sense of accomplishment is the result.

Many benefits are derived from communicating and maintaining this level of mental clarity and awareness. In daily life, there is less surprise confrontation. The reaction or response to a situation is constructive, not destructive. Thus, a better sense of control over the immediate environment is gained, which empowers the individual to trust in nature. All individuals would benefit by developing such a heightened state of awareness.

• • •

BODY, MIND, AND SPIRIT UNIFICATION

There are three levels of understanding the unification of the body, mind, and spirit:

1. Body, or the physical level of understanding *(this chapter)*.
2. Mind, or the intellectual level of understanding *(next chapter)*.
3. Spirit, or the deep, spiritual level of understanding *(Part Four, Satori)*.

The physical level of understanding is simplified by one basic example: reading. It is a practice in which everyone eventually engages in. In fact, you are doing it right now. To begin reading, the first thing you do is find a comfortable chair or couch. Many of you probably have a favorite reading chair which, I'm sure, is broken in, like your favorite saddle, in all the right places. Next, have something to sip on and maybe some munchies, too. Do not forget to put the phone nearby to avoid having to move. Better yet, turn on the answering machine and forget the phone. That way, you can engage your whole being in your book. What did we forget? Ah, yes. The book. Let us begin.

First, your body must hold the book steady in order for your eyes to focus on the printed words. This is involvement, coordination, and immersion of the physical aspect of yourself in what you are doing.

Second, your intellect must be held steady, unwavering in intensity, not allowing any outside distractions. In this way, the mind can grasp the meaning of what is being read. This is involvement, coordination, and immersion of the mind or intellectual aspect of yourself into what you are doing.

Third, your heart must be filled with a desire or motivation to grasp the writer's intended meaning of the words your mind is processing. This is involvement, coordination, and immersion of the emotional aspect of yourself into what you are doing.

Lastly, your "soul" must be filled with sincerity to not only learn, but also be positively and constructively transformed by what you are doing. This way, your efforts will not be in vain. This is involvement, coordination, and immersion of the spiritual aspect of your being.

If any of these four essential components of human existence is not involved toward this one effort of reading the book, we will be unable to understand what is being communicated, and all efforts are wasted. This applies universally to any situation or endeavor.

Equestrian art demands concentration and unification of body, mind, spirit, and soul. Unless this takes place, we may be deluding ourselves into thinking that we are directing our efforts into the perfection of an art form. In reality, we are merely sitting on top of the horse in what appears to be horseback riding.

. . .

All things in nature abide by natural law, including human understanding and growth. This is demonstrated by the circle of human potential.

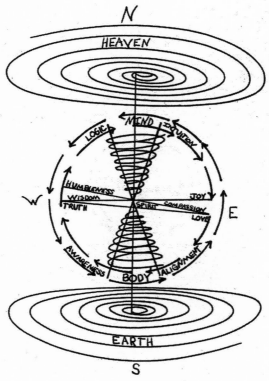

CIRCLE OF HUMAN POTENTIAL
Illustration F

When all three aspects of being: body, mind and spirit, align, universal energy ignites at the core of existence or center of gravity. The energy patterns are focused and united to connect and expand with external *ki*. The virtues of love, compassion, joy, humbleness, truth and spiritual wisdom are interrelated at this point of combustion. The four directions of north, south, east and west maintain balance within the individual as the external *ki* supports the movement. The human body is the manifestation of the emotional and spiritual well-being of the soul.

• • •

There are three phases to personal transformation. First, physical training and self-discipline in a given field. Next, study and contemplate to develop a sound moral and ethical foundation or personal philosophy. Last, there occurs a systematic unconscious manifestation of the fruits of this effort toward personal transformation.

Each time this cycle is repeated, a greater understanding and insight into the value of human transformation is gained. It can be complex when approached on an intellectual level, but it is extremely simple when undertaken with a strong, sincere desire for self-improvement and understanding. This understanding of the basic, yet profound nature of life and self is its own reward.

In Eastern cultures, this struggle toward self-discipline and inner balance is readily understood as a pathway to self-realization. Eastern philosophy describes the body, mind and spirit separation from the beginning of creation as a division or split of the one-energy of realism, forming an ostensible duality. This duality or partition, right and wrong, male and female, and other pairs of opposites, are one and the same, like two sides of a coin, but appear different or separate to us because of the nature of the brain.

The brain is divided into a right and a left hemisphere. Each hemisphere tends to function separately from the other. In most individuals, this separation is unbalanced or linear, meaning only one side of the brain is utilized at any given time. Because of this linear thinking, the universe is viewed as separate, rather than the universe of Oneness. If the two sides of the brain balance and function simultaneously, enlightenment occurs.

Scientific brain research indicates that intense concentration causes a proportionate degree of brain synchronization. This is called focus. (*Part Three, Concentration.*) Three basic stages are experienced as the brain begins to synchronize. The first one is the Alpha brain wave. This is the state just before sleep. If awake, an individual experiences a mild, meditative state. The second stage, called Theta or dream state, is activated. This stage is a deeper meditative state.

Further synchronization enters one into the third stage called the Delta brain wave state or deep, dreamless sleep. Delta waves also occur in extremely deep states of meditation. Modern scientific research thus gives a physiological basis for the spiritual process of enlightenment.

This process of inner unification and balance is vital to understanding and eliminating the paradoxical nature of life. This elimination of duality and the emergence of non-differentiation is called Oneness. To reach this point of detachment or Oneness, the three phases of personal transformation must be developed equally, simultaneously, and systematically.

Let us simplify this: Take the colors black and white. If they remain separate, they are simply black and white, and only have the potential of black or white alone. If they are mixed you have gray. This is neutral. There is no separation or division between the two. Instead the blending created a middle line or neutral area. One side is not weighted more than the other. The two are centered. In order to remain centered, they must become one. During the blending process, gray gained the potential of itself, plus black and white.

Synchronizing the body, mind and spirit strengthens and builds harmony within the individual. When this occurs, the body is no longer disconnected from the mind and spirit. Previously, it was it's own entity. Synchronization allows the mind to control the body instead of the contrary.

The mind is not in the future or past, but in the present moment, fully capable and ready to concentrate on the task at hand. It gives the orders, and the body responds willingly.

The spirit becomes the guiding light. It has a direction or goal to aim for. The body and mind cooperate to get the task done with ease and harmony. All three aspects of self are engaged in this one purpose at the present moment. This process allows synchronization to occur.

Equestrian art encompasses these three phases of personal transformation: physical, mental and emotional conditioning. A rider matures by constant, focused effort, diligent physical training, and mental discipline. This is personal transformation. The goal is construction, not instruction. The goal is transformation, not information.

The beginner lives in a world of insecurity. There is limited physical balance and mental flexibility. As the rider pursues his practice, insecurity dissolves. Efforts are transformed into self-confidence, and the rider relaxes physically, mentally, and spiritually.

On occasion, the beginner experiences a glimpse of synchronization of the body and mind, therefore, connecting briefly with the rhythm of the horse. This is the occasional but unpredictable "I got it," and the rider is filled with bliss.

In that split second, Oneness is experienced. The body, mind, and subconscious take note of this rare experience of synchronicity. On a nonintellectual level of understanding, the rider is driven to seek this level of awareness again. Over time, the rider becomes aware of how personal transformation leads to body, mind and spiritual unity. From this standpoint, a rider learns to ride from a sincere desire for self-improvement and understanding.

Much of the time this inner transformation occurs beyond an intellectual level. If this practice is pursued beyond a level of attachment to the physical experience of sport, any rider can transform riding into an art form, and attain body, mind and spiritual unity.

. . .

PART TWO
BODY

. . .

INTRODUCTION

A balanced rider focuses attention on the body: this includes posture, awareness of tension, body position, and their influence on the horse. Focusing attention on these aspects of the body quickly reveals a misaligned body structure. This also influences the carriage of the horse. By improving our posture, it is easy to recognize the interrelationship between the correct posture of the rider and the balanced carriage of the horse. Correct posture and balance are one of the essential ingredients in becoming a balanced rider.

The balance of your body and mind reflects outward in your posture, breath and movement. Training the body as well as the mind insures a well-balanced approach to self-development. Physical training develops the body, while mental discipline develops the mind.

For example: When reading a book, the body should be engaged with the task of body awareness in addition to mental concentration. Reading is thus transformed into training, and at the same time, integrates body and mind. Integration increases our ability to maintain balance, posture, stability, and alignment because the mind is focused. Stability of the mind improves as well as strength of character (spirit). In every action, the entire body should be unified. To train one aspect of the body, mind, or spirit, relationship creates imbalance and disharmony.

The benefits of good posture and balance are incorporated into daily life. Clarity of mind is restored by focused efforts. This allows for the body and mind to become stable and remain that way, even in adverse situations. In this condition, the individual is naturally calm, and physically fit. Stability and adaptability to circumstances improves markedly. The natural results are whole body movement, balance and connection.

Training the body develops consciousness (mind), increasing your humanity (spirit). This is why body and mind are interrelated in all disciplines.

Before engaging in any activity for the purpose of self-improvement, three things must be practiced ritually:

1. Adjust the posture.
2. Empty the mind.
3. Adjust the breath.

Equestrian art nurtures these three aspects of self-development, creating a balanced environment that complies with natural law.

• • •

BODY AWARENESS

The horse is the reflection of the rider. A crooked rider presents a crooked horse. The extent to which the rider has developed a keen sense of body awareness is shown in the carriage of the horse.

Focused attention on body position and alignment enables the rider to feel and correct misalignments in his body, thereby simultaneously correcting the carriage of the horse. If a rider is to maintain balance and impulsion within the energetic strides of the horse, this sense of self-adjustment is a necessity.

For example: If the horse is holding on to the bit, pulling, and showing a tense jaw-line and poll, the rider most likely is grinding his teeth, locking the jaw and back of the neck, perhaps even the shoulders. The wrists and forearms come into play. In the majority of cases, they are locked and pulling on the reins because the rider is not balanced in the seat. The rider has disengaged connectivity with the seat and leg aids, preventing the horse from traveling forward through the topline to the bit.

The natural rhythm and cycle of energy is interrupted, creating tension in the body and mind. At this point, the rider loses the ability to interpret the reactions of the horse. A tense mind clouds communication with the horse. To reestablish connectivity and clear the mind, the rider needs to let go and take a breath. *(Part Four, Breath.)*

Taking a deep breath encourages relaxation. In this circumstance, letting go and breathing naturally unlocks the jaw, as well as the neck, shoulders and wrists. The center of gravity drops, allowing the rider to sit deeper in the saddle and apply the proper leg aids. Hence, the horse moves forward and up into the rider's hands, instead of against them.

This subtle correction simultaneously alters the carriage of the horse. This is called *sympathetic vibration*, which means the reaction of the horse is triggered by the vibration of the rider's body, creating a sympathetic body carriage. The horse easily reflects back to the rider the tension and misalignment of the rider's own posture.

Through sympathetic vibration, a rider who remains attuned to body position and alignment can correct a mis-carriage of the horse by first making the adjustments in his own position.

Let's say you are in the middle of a riding lesson and the instructor says, "Unlock your inside shoulder." The instructor proceeds to explain that the horse is having a hard time using its shoulder because your shoulder is locked, which in turn is displacing your inside seat-bone and hips, thus preventing proper use of leg and seat aids. The horse becomes sympathetic, mimicking your body posture by falling in on its haunches, not being able to step under with its inside hind leg because it can't drop the inside hip. He bulges against your inside leg and hangs on the inside rein while planting himself on the forehand or inside shoulder.

You try desperately to make the correction. It just doesn't seem to happen. Weeks pass; suddenly, you notice the horse is traveling more forward and you don't feel your shoulder and hip so displaced. You stopped focusing on the problem and your natural instinct took control. Doing so allowed a natural realignment of your body position. The results show by the unrestricted movement and complacent attitude of your horse. At last, he can give you the correct bend with little effort. For him, it becomes a joy when you allow him the space.

Be an active participant in your character development, and reap strength from self-discipline. You have earned it. To do this, a rider simply needs to understand and accept this fact: The horse is a reflection of its rider. This is the first important step to physical awareness. The second step involves application to daily life.

Everyday, we drive a car, or at least most people do. Much time is spent sitting at traffic lights and in traffic jams. This is the perfect opportunity to practice body awareness and improve as a rider. Let us say you are traveling at about thirty-five miles per hour. You are approaching a left turn on a downgrade, two-lane road. There are no cars approaching in the opposite direction. Your signal light goes on, and you prepare to make the turn. What happens?

Normally, the whole body shifts position and leans to one side, as if the body is turning the car. In most cases, the head leads, then the sloping shoulder and forearms, followed by the seat.

Back at the stable, you are riding along the short side of the arena. Your left leg is the inside leg. You ask your horse to bend into the outside rein and come off the rail by using your outside right leg, while maintaining the bend with the left inside leg to make a perfect twenty-meter circle.

Is this really what happens? Not always. Most likely, we make a round circle the same way we turn the corner in the car. The whole body shifts as we try to make a round circle with our heads, followed by sloping shoulders, and pulling on the inside rein, as if it was a steering wheel. Is it any wonder our horses even make some resemblance of a circle? They sure give it their best effort, despite the misalignment of the passenger they carry.

Improve your circle by practicing turns while driving. Do this by applying body awareness. Concentrate on maintaining correct body position, from the seat bones up to the head. Keep the head up and centered over the spine, allowing the vertebrae to stack in alignment. The body remains square, meaning shoulders and hips are aligned. Do not collapse the abdomen as you bend into the turn. Instead, remain upright, with your lower back pressed against the seat back. This keeps you centered as the car takes the turn. If standing, the feet would be one shoulder width apart. With this alignment, all other body parts fall into place.

Note the position of your seat and the muscles involved to maintain that position throughout the turn. They are the same muscles utilized in riding a half halt. It is a bracing of the back. Make a conscious effort to look through the turn in the direction headed. Be careful not to ride the turn ahead of the horse, or in this example, prepare your body to make the turn ahead of the car.

Less energy is expended, and with enough practice, this awareness begins to correct your position on the horse by changing the habitual posture. With sincere effort, the horse eventually is allowed to make a round circle, instead of you trying to do it for him.

Let's ride again. Where are your eyes focused while riding? The most common position is hypnotized and looking down at the poll or ears of the horse. This can be called "fixation." The focus is on one object and does not allow vision of the surrounding environment. At this point, body awareness is stifled.

Fixation of the mind causes inner movement to stop. The rider's breath becomes shallow and stops intermittently. This hinders movement of energy, thus preventing relaxation and unification of the body, mind, and spirit. Once this happens, there is no interaction with the environment. The unwanted tension disengages the rider from the inner rhythm of the horse. Looking up and away from the poll and ears of the horse alters the focus of the mind. The eyes, no longer "fixed" in one position, soften and allow the rider to relax and breathe.

Eyes that "see all" bring alertness or awareness to the activity currently engaged in. Participation increases to the level of *zanchin*. Remember *zanchin*? It is an applied alertness and state of readiness to the environment. (*Part One, Communication*). Not allowing "fixation" leads to a state of *mushin*, or no mind. (*Part Three, No Mind*).

Developing eyes that "see all" can be practiced on a daily basis. While driving, look up and far ahead in the distance. Keep your eyes alert while scanning the surrounding environment. Do not allow them to become fixed in one direction. You can always tell when this happens. It is a dead stare. You may even ride pass your exit on the freeway.

A conscious reminder or awareness of "fixation" is needed to alter the pattern of habit and allow you to ride by looking through and above the horse's ears. This elevates the forehand of the horse and frees its shoulders, making it much easier to make a round circle. It is easier to direct the horse because looking where you are going creates the thought of where you want to go. The mind activates the body into action. The body responds instantaneously, with the proper aids. Receptivity to outside stimulus improves as the mind becomes flexible and moving. It's easy; just think it.

Enough driving for one day . . . how about sitting or walking? You are about to sit down and watch TV after a hard day at the office. Do you plop yourself down on top of the chair, or do you sit lightly on the chair? When mounting your horse, do you plop into the saddle or sit lightly? How about walking from the parking lot to the store. Are your shoulders sloping, head leading, and eyes focused on the ground? If you are thinking, nine times out of ten they are. (*Illustration A, Part Two, Body Alignment.*) This is a common posture.

Let us not quit yet. I think you are understanding the importance of daily body awareness in relation to riding your horse. Do you feel the weight of your body in your heels? Most of the time, the weight is on the ball of your foot, or partially in the heel. The weight should be equally balanced on your foot.

Look at the bottom of your shoes the same way you look at your horse's shoe or hoof to see how it is balanced and worn. Normally, the heel of your shoe is worn on one side or the other; it is not balanced. Wearing high-heeled shoes throws the weight onto the ball of the foot, and it becomes difficult to feel any weight in the heel. Once the weight relaxes into the heel, you begin to walk softly on the ground, just as you begin to sit into your horse.

Riding instructors are always using the term "drop your weight to your heels." How can this be done if an individual cannot sit into a chair or walk into the earth? It is simple if you apply this concept in daily life. Practicing to sit properly in a chair carries over to sitting deep in the saddle and dropping the weight of the body into the heels. Conscious control of body parts allows the center of gravity to be lowered.

Conscious control develops lightness of the body. Most riders should know the importance of lightness of the body. Let me help you with it. Lightness is what provides the carrying energy of the horse. If you think heavy thoughts, your body becomes heavy. This acts like an anchor, pulling the horse down even if you ask it to move forward.

Gravity and relaxation of the tensions held in the muscles drop the weight into the heels, not force. A simple thought can send the energy to the heels, dropping the weight. This allows the leg to relax and lengthen naturally. Most individuals carry too much energy in the upper body. *(Illustration A, Part Two, Body Alignment.)* The thought releases the stale energy and directs it to your place of intention. *(Part Four, Life Force Energy.)* With this release of energy, comes lightness.

A good example of lightness is reflected in any wild animal. Observe how they interact with the surrounding environment. They possess power, agility, and harmony. The impression left on the earth is shallow and light, not deep and heavy. They walk into the earth, not on it, while still maintaining connectivity with nature. They appear to be light.

Have you ever seen a wild animal full of tension and knots? No. They sit, totally relaxed and complacent; but at any moment, they can readily spring into action without injury to muscles.

This type of elasticity and harmony is nurtured by lightness. Lightness comes from practicing body awareness. Lightness is a key element to bringing balance of body, mind, and spirit, while improving as a rider.

Developing body awareness has many benefits. A simple thought becomes an interaction with the world around you. Awareness and connectivity of the surrounding environment increases twofold. The feeling of being an innocent victim to circumstance dissipates because of a newfound understanding of the nature of things.

Body awareness begins the construction of a strong foundation. This foundation is built on natural law. Equestrian art is built on the same foundation.

. . .

BODY ALIGNMENT

When a rider sits correctly aligned, the rider's center of gravity and body position on the horse is supportive. This enables correct use of all aids and freedom of movement in the horse. Any leaning sideways, forward, or backward displaces the alignment and center of gravity for horse and rider. This basic alignment is required to influence the horse effectively and with little effort. If one area of the body is out of alignment, another area compensates.

The correct position of the rider dictates that the ear, shoulder, hip and heel be aligned. This alignment supports the restacking of the major sections of the body by bringing the head, shoulders, chest, pelvis and legs toward a more vertical or upright position. It lengthens the body to approach the ideal position for the rider. The left and right sides of the body are equally balanced, and the pelvis sits horizontally, allowing the weight of the trunk to fall directly over the center of gravity. Translated to riding, it allows the rider to sit with equal weight distribution on both sides of the saddle and deliver effective riding aids.

The body weight of most individuals has shifted away from the natural alignment. During this shift, the muscles and ligaments may twist or shorten as the body slouches. The head protrudes forward in front of the vertical axis and may even tilt to one side as the shoulders curl inward *(Illustration A)*. This is also a common posture in the saddle.

Unnoticed, the misalignment continues as the body compensates. Eventually, one shoulder and hip leads the other in walking or one shoulder and seat-bone is lower than the other while riding. As the torso reshapes, the knees may turn in or out, putting extra weight on the legs, feet and spine. This interferes with the gait while walking. For the rider it becomes difficult to keep the toes straight in the stirrups with the heels down and knees pointed forward. There is difficulty with lengthening the leg because the distribution of weight on the seatbones is unequal and the twist in the knees prevents the legs from draping naturally around the horse.

This instability of the lower body or center of gravity throws the weight of the upper body to the inside or outside of the saddle and either forward or away from the center of gravity of the horse. For the rider, one leg may be longer than the other, and one side may be heavier. It becomes difficult to maintain the correct body alignment on the horse because the natural vertical alignment has become distorted.

There are many reasons for this reshaping of the human body. For one, the connective tissue or fascia surrounding the muscles of the body is pliable, making it a moldable part of the body. It can easily be reshaped by environmental factors and stored emotional energy, such as pain, hurt, and negative emotions. This energy deposits in the fascia as a muscle memory, creating unwanted tension in the musculature of the body. These tensions contract the muscles, causing an imbalance from one side of the body to the other. The individual compensates and shifts the carriage of weight. Should this imbalance continue for a period of time, the natural vertical alignment of the body becomes reshaped as previously described.

Mishaps, for example, can cause the reshaping of the physical and emotional body; such as a fall from a horse that twists a knee or hip joint causing a limp for a few weeks. The weight shift onto the strong leg adds more stress not only to the legs, but also to the support system of the entire body. Although the limp disappears as the injury heals and strengthens, the areas of compensation leave its impression as a misaligned body.

Emotional energy directly affects the connective tissue and alters body alignment. An overly critical mother or father is an example of an affecting energy on the alignment of the body. In this example, fear of being hurt or fear of rejection keeps the individual from expressing the innermost feelings. As a result, the chest caves in or closes down as a way of self-protection. The chest is the seat of the heart chakra, or energy center. *(Part Four, Life Force)* The fear causes the heart center to retreat and the head and mind come forward, leading the way.

The misalignment becomes more pronounced as the shoulders slope forward. Future heartbreaking experiences cause the chest to depress or collapse even more. A depressed heart center separates the body, mind and spirit, preventing the individual from feeling or experiencing love. Concaving the chest gives an individual a false sense of security and protection from further hurt and pain in this area of the body.

When this happens, an individual subconsciously learns to use the head and mind to experience and interpret reality, as opposed to the body, mind, and spirit collectively. This sequence of structural change continues and eventually, the abdomen collapses. The abdominal muscle is the primary muscle responsible for holding us up. It corresponds with self-support, or taking responsibility for one's life.

Restructuring of the body builds a habitual posture. The head leads, the body slumps, while the mind tries to figure out and control things instead of feeling and letting go. *(Illustration A.)* Fear dictates the normal response to daily stimuli. The mind is convinced that the body cannot support the emotional state of being. This pattern of body carriage becomes the normal balance for an individual. The muscular reshaping and emotional energy are of the same origin.

Emotional energy deposits tension in different areas of the body. Tension in the muscles manipulated by massage or other therapeutic bodywork can trigger an emotional response or memory. The normal reaction is to tighten up or pull away to protect this area. What is being protected is the emotional energy that has been stored in the tissue. Letting go of the emotion associated with pain allows the muscle to relax and enables the therapist to re-shape the body and encourage more elasticity within the connective tissue.

Misalignments and reshaping of the body can cause the muscles to take on the weight-bearing function of the skeletal system. If this continues for any length of time, the muscle tissue develops the same hard, immovable quality of bone. Eventually, this becomes infectious; the body locks up, and the joints lose their freedom of movement. The body parts are disorganized from one another and the individual loses flexibility and suppleness.

Symptoms such as weakness, discomfort, pain, lack of motivation and emotional instability develop. The entire body including the internal organs and circulatory system are affected by the misalignment. Blood flow is constricted due to the hardened and reshaped muscular tissue. The depression of the upper chest limits respiration. Crookedness and slouching displaces internal organs. The legs develop swelling or pain due to abnormal pressure in the pelvic region. Chronic tension permanently shortens the connective tissue. This new shape replaces the normal way of functioning for the body. Realignment at this point is uncomfortable because the reshaped body carriage is now recorded as the correct one.

Let's take this to the arena. A rider with a tilted pelvic places more weight on one seat-bone than the other. One shoulder is lower, and one leg is longer. One hand is carried slightly higher than the other, and the head is cocked to the left or right.

To balance the body, the rider has to adjust the center of gravity to equalize the added weight, let's say on the left side. Because of this shift in the center of gravity, the left side of the body will be heavier than the right side. There is an imbalance in the load. Applied to the horse, the reaction is to drop the left hip and shoulder lower than the right, and perhaps hang on the left rein for balance because the rider's left hand is lower than the right, thus, nagging the horse. It is that subtle.

The body of a horse experiences similar misalignments and shortening of connective tissue as the rider's. In most cases, an improperly fitted saddle, poor training, abusive riding, hoof imbalance, confinement, trauma, or a lack of love from handlers causes this shortening or misalignment.

A horse that is not ridden forward with the driving power

from its hindquarters experiences shortening of the connective tissue. It becomes uncomfortable for the horse to lengthen its stride because of the shortened fascia. The horse feels the muscles pull as it tries to lengthen its stride. It hesitates or breaks gait. Through proper schooling, the tissues are reshaped to allow suppleness, and the horse relearns the right feel.

Continuous riding on the forehand causes the muscles of the shoulders to shorten. This creates difficulty with elevation and lateral movements. Shortened muscle tissue of the shoulders restricts the horse from crossing deep with the front legs for lateral movements. The amount of restriction is determined by the amount of driving with the hindquarters.

If there is not enough impulsion from the hindquarters of the horse, there will be a lack of elevation. Lack of elevation restricts the amount of depth to the lateral movement. To obtain freedom of movement in each stride of the horse and lengthen the connective tissue, the horse must be driven from the hindquarters, and not from the forehand.

Shortening of the neck muscles is another common fault in the carriage of the horse. An unbalanced or inexperienced rider seeking to create a frame or gain contact with the bit resorts to setting the "head position" of the horse with the hands.

Instead, what happens is, the rider's pelvis is tipped back or sitting on the crotch. The abdomen and chest collapse. Sometimes, these postures occur in unison. This position of the rider throws the center of gravity forward. The seat-bones thus come off the saddle, and the lower back locks, restricting movement in the seat. The rider grabs with the knees, causing the lower leg to come off the horse. The rider now has difficulty maintaining leg contact and most likely resorts to kicking the horse to urge him forward. The rider becomes heavy and sends the driving energy down to the earth like a weight. *(Illustration C.)* This is called riding on the forehand.

In an effort to regain balance, the rider pulls the horse's neck up and in. The reins are used to replace the poor balance in the seat. This is abusive use of the hands. Out of self-protection, the horse shortens the neck, giving a "head position." Many riders are fooled into believing the horse is on the bit with this given "head position." In actuality, the horse's back is locked. He balances on the reins and becomes a leg mover. The carriage of the horse imitates the carriage of the rider. This is sympathetic vibration, remember?

If there is no forward action of the hindquarters, there cannot be contact with the bit. To lengthen the fascia of a horse that has been ridden in this position, the rider first needs to adjust and realign his body, beginning with the seat.

The rider re-establishes his center of gravity by repositioning his body to align with the center of gravity of his mount. The rest of the body follows suit and allows the rider effective communication with the leg and seat aids. Proper use of the leg and seat aids drive the horse from the hindquarters into the rein's contact, with less effort.

Lengthening of the topline helps to lighten the forehand and free up the shoulders, while connecting the hindquarters to the forehand. This can be accomplished by allowing the horse to stretch forward on a long rein and reach for the ground. The fascia can now be reshaped, and the horse is able to comply with a balanced carriage. The forward rhythm maintains contact with the bit and aligns the horse, not by excessive use of the hands. Riding the horse on the forehand is perhaps the major cause of misalignment and ill temper in horses.

Over the years, patterns of misalignment reinforce themselves; they become comfortable and natural. This deepens by repetition and therefore, when making adjustments, there is rebellion in a horse or a man. The body refuses to cooperate with the mind. The correct posture is replaced with a reshaped body carriage, and the mind registers the reshaping as correct.

This pattern of imbalance is often experienced when a green rider and an unruly horse are paired. The rider considers the irregular gait or misbehavior of the horse as normal. Any change to reestablish fluidity and balance in the horse will seem uncomfortable since the old way of traveling is engraved in the memory. This is where someone with a trained eye is most helpful. A comment heard often is, "Oh, he always travels like that." The habit is reinforced by repetition. Habitual repetition of a preferred posture creates individualized tension patterns and begins to be a comforting habit, like putting on a favorite jacket. Eventually, this posture becomes dominant, and the realignment more difficult.

The horse, too, rebels to the retraining of his body carriage. Like you, the horse has preferred postures and habits that are comfortable and become more dominant. He does not like being asked to do something that requires use of muscles that have become dormant and shortened.

The process is a gradual lengthening of the fascia and reshaping of the musculature of the horse. During the reshaping or retraining process, the rider must request more action from the hindquarters of the horse. It feels uncomfortable to the horse, not only because of the shortened fascia, but because a shortened carriage has become an ingrained habit or way of traveling. The discomfort and stress of having to use the dormant muscles creates resistance from the horse. This resistance comes in a way such as bucking, running faster, tossing the head, stomping, or a temper tantrum, or a combination thereof. Keep this in mind to alleviate problems that may arise during the process of realigning your horse. The aches and discomforts of your horse are the only way the horse can communicate his efforts to you.

To be effective, the rider needs to be aligned and listening to the rhythmatic sound of the horse in motion. The simplest way to achieve this is to allow the body to remember. Riding requires a lengthening of the rider's body to enable the legs and seat to be positioned in the horse's center of gravity. The connective tissue of the rider is reshaped to this new position. The realignment of the major body sections nurtures balance in the rider. The building blocks of the body support each other equally.

To sustain a forward-moving collected trot, the rider is lifted in the abdomen, and the spine lengthens and raises the same as the horse's spine. *(Sympathetic Vibration.)* The rider allows room for the horse to suspend and bring his back up under the seat of the rider. At the same time, the rider is suspended in motion within the rhythm of the horse. This is lightness. *(See Body Awareness).*

The expulsion of the horse lifts the body, developing into a more balanced seat by strengthening the *hara*. *(Part Four, Breath.)*

A rigid posture does not allow freedom of movement in either partner. A balanced seat allows the body to remember. The rider constantly readjusts his position and alignment in the saddle to remain balanced while maintaining alignment of the horse. This is an effective rider.

Ask only of your horse what you ask of yourself. Here we go— more body awareness. This time, bring awareness to the alignment of your body. How crooked are you? When you sit, do you sit straight in the chair, with feet flat on the floor? Nine times out of ten, the body is slouched to one side, legs are crossed, and the body is leaning on the arm of the chair. Be honest. Remember plopping into the chair to watch TV? Check your seat-bones. They are important for riding. Is your weight balanced equally on your seat-bones? This does not mean rigid. The seat should be relaxed and balanced. When you walk, does your chin and head lead first, and your feet drag behind? If so, the body is poorly aligned. *(Illustration A.)* This sounds like the same things we ask the horse not to do, which is get off the forehand.

The horse is required to carry itself forward, meaning driving from the hindquarters, or from the back to the front of the horse with a supple and supportive topline, responsiveness to the aids of the rider and tracking straight. This aligns the spinal column of the horse and allows a natural re-alignment or adjustment while remaining in self-carriage and balance. The forehand lightens, the shoulders unlock, and the jaw softens allowing an expression of effortlessness in the movement of the horse. This natural progression of alignment is true for individuals also. Do not wait until you need to ride again before you work on your alignment. This can be practiced while walking.

Believe it or not, walking helps realign your horse. How? By realigning yourself. Concentrate on placing your feet under your body and step forward, as if you were a horse. Take a long stride. This encourages the use of your buttocks. Eventually, the abdomen lifts and supports the body. Once the abdomen lifts, it is much easier to open the chest and bring the shoulders back naturally. The head falls into alignment in a progressive stacking of body parts. There is connectivity not only within the body, but also with the surrounding environment. *(Illustration B.)* Movement is initiated from the center of gravity. Realignment unfolds as the body remembers how good it feels to be straight. Daily effort and conscious commitment aligns the body and mind by changing your walk.

When the walk changes, an evolutionary process of synchronization of the body and mind occurs. Your efforts will be reflected in the carriage of the horse.

. . .

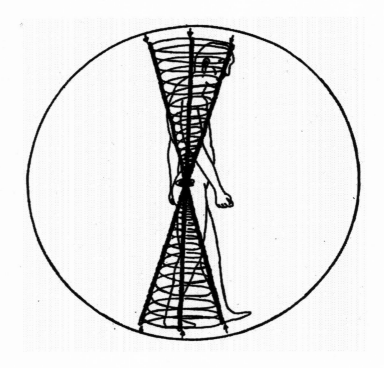

CIRCLE OF DISPLACEMENT
Illustration A

The circle represents universal energy. The top of the circle is heaven, representing vision, and the bottom is earth, representing stability. This illustration shows a lack of heaven-and-earth connectivity. The energy traveling the spine does not have a direct connection with universal energy. Consequently, the lines of force are dispersed through the upper body, creating a heavy brain. The *hara* is sheltered and disconnected from the earth's magnetic force. There is a lack of clarity because of deficient earth grounding. The mind is leading, or on the forehand, the body lacks balance, and the feet and legs are trailing behind. Back problems and displacement will most likely arise from this type of misalignment.

• • •

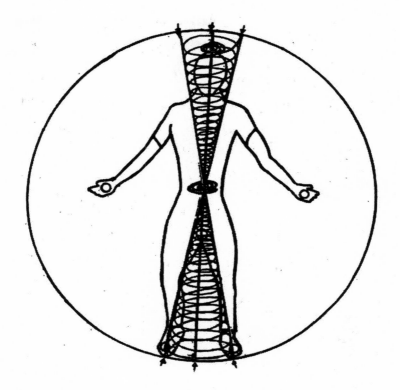

CIRCLE OF CENTEREDNESS
Illustration B-1

This demonstrates the importance of body alignment. Here, universal energy, represented by the circle, is received from heaven and earth. The lines of force are in direct balance with the Earth's magnetic force. Heaven's energy travels down the spine, and earth's energy travels up the spine to meet in the *hara*, or the center of gravity. Points of entry are the palms of the hands, soles and top of the feet, base of the spine, and top of the head. The feet are in line with the shoulders. The body walks, acts, and thinks in balance and clarity. All movement is initiated from the *hara*. With this alignment, you have self-carriage.

• • •

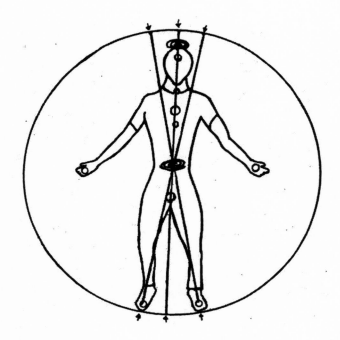

CIRCLE OF CENTEREDNESS
Illustration B-2

Within this circle of centeredness, alignment of the chakra centers or energy vortexes are activated. This assists in aligning the physical body to the purpose of the spiritual body, encouraging the evolution of the soul. There are seven major centers: the crown or 1st vortex, located at the top of the head, represents the connection to universal consciousness. Third eye or brow chakra, in the center of the forehead, is the source of inner vision and communication. Throat or 3rd vortex is the center for projection of choices. Heart chakra, located in the center of the chest, represents unconditional love. Solar Plexus or 5th vortex is the feeling center. Navel is the center of balance and life issues. The root chakra, located at the base of the spine, governs how stable or grounded one is in the physical life.

. . .

Walking, sitting, standing, carrying objects, lifting and so on, can be looked upon as training of the body and mind. We constantly carry things. Practice carrying them in balance and maintain alignment. If the tendency is to carry things in the right hand and on the right side, the outcome is lopsidedness.

In an effort to balance the added weight, the left hip and left shoulder drops. The pelvic tilts upward on the right side and downward on the left side. Consequently, an imbalance in the horse is created also. The horse will carry his left hip lower because of the added weight of the rider's lower hip. His left shoulder will drop to the inside, and he will have a tendency to hang on to the left rein for balance.

Riding on the right rein, the rider's right hip will be higher than the left hip. The horse will short-stride on the right inside hind leg and avoid stepping forward and under his body with the right leg. He will have difficulty bending on a circle while traveling to the right.

Practice body alignment by carrying items in balance. Place objects in your center of gravity and remain in alignment. Maintain balance by stilling your weight and stepping forward with a long stride. This activates the *hara* and stills the hands, an important criterion for balanced riding.

Achievements show as improved posture and a more positive outlook. Normally, the body acquires a lift, or lightness, as the head goes up, the chest opens and the arms fall naturally in place. The trunk of the body lengthens and the pelvis becomes horizontal, allowing the abdominal muscles to support the rest of the body. This enables the weight of the torso to be distributed equally over the hip joints and legs. The equal weight distribution encourages an even stride with less fluctuation of the body from side to side, and less rising up and down with each step. Fewer injuries occur because the muscles are moveable with increased range of flexibility. Energy is conserved for other purposes.

The horse experiences a similar structural change that results in greater freedom and elasticity of movement, increased elevation, longer strides, and forward movement. The horse is happy to perform, as it is now easier for him.

Body alignment not only affects you and your horse, but also your daily interaction with others. For instance, every four to six weeks, you need a haircut, unless you like the shaggy type of haircut. You plop yourself down in the haircutting chair and slouch to one side. Your legs are crossed, thus dropping the hip and shoulder and throwing the seat-bones to one side. Believe it or not, this affects the outcome of your haircut. The hairdresser does not perceive your head properly because it is out of alignment with the rest of the body. The hair is cut to the present misaligned position of your body. Sometimes, the results can be disastrous.

An individual's first impression comes from the way we present ourselves to the public. Meaning, a subconscious thought of how we feel is transmitted through automatic acuity. The body represents how we think and feel. It is the outward manifestation of our innermost truths.

Body expression is determined by body alignment and mental clarity. Posture reflects self-acceptance or denial. Self-acceptance encompasses such traits as discipline, responsibility, humbleness and motivation. This is normally reflected as a tall, aligned body carriage, regardless of the height of the individual. Self-denial encompasses traits such as dishonesty with self and others, lack of responsibility, and a general weakness of character. A short, slumped body carriage generally demonstrates this type of emotional thought form. *(Illustrations 1,2.3,4)*

Body alignment builds its foundation on body awareness and sympathetic vibration. Proper alignment of the rider supports and maintains the rhythm of the horse in a forward-moving, energetic gait. Good posture encourages body, mind and spiritual alignment. From this, a great sense of wellness permeates your being.

. . .

EFFECTS OF BODY EXPRESSION
ON THE HORSE

FORCEFUL
Illustration 1

This individual experiences the need to control and challenge the horse. He refuses to be humiliated by anyone or anything, in this case, the horse. Unconsciously, this position communicates, "Notice me!" There is a constant battle of wills between the rider and the horse. Stiffness makes it hard for the rider to have a supple seat and to elongate his legs. For this rider it is much easier to use brawn instead of finesse and the horse is manhandled in an effort to gain control.

The hands, instead of the seat, initiate all riding. The horse is controlled by assertion of body postures, such as stiffness, pulling up and back in a position of conceit and challenge. This type of rider would require a patient and willing horse that succumbs to the demands placed on it. The need for control is greater than humbleness and the skill to ride harmoniously.

To become a proficient rider, the ego must be humble enough to step aside. This can be hard for this type of individual. It requires swallowing of pride; only then can the individual absorb what the horse has to teach.

. . .

UNYIELDING
Illustration 2

"I'm insecure, so don't push me," is the subconscious message this body type delivers.

Because of this "immovable" attitude, the horse struggles to be free, possibly by running away with the rider. To improve as a rider, this individual must learn to bend and compromise.

The restrictive anatomy makes it difficult to open the hips and move with the horse. Stiffness is the result. The natural rhythm of the horse is restrained by the seat, legs and hands of the rider. The horse is asked to go forward, yet the restraint from the rider prevents this action. Contradictory signals are sent to the horse, creating confusion. This rider has a tendency to lock his hands into a fixed position, therefore preventing the horse from stretching forward and taking contact with the bit.

This type of individual likes everything his way. If they are ready to give a little, it is done cautiously, making sure the reward follows. Being accepted is where the effort goes, but the tendency is to betray the self by denying the acceptance. This type of rider cannot ride a horse that is nervous or sensitive, unless the emotional attitude changes.

• • •

ENGULFING
Illustration 3

As a rider, this body type smothers the horse. The horse is ridden as if it were a possession or a precious artifact. The nurturing attitude provides a good home for the horse, but this type can never ride the horse to its fullest potential. The need to "look pretty or elegant" is foremost in the mind of the individual. The horse is ridden by engulfing it with the rider's body and suffocating it as they try to "get into" the horse, so to speak.

At times, the movement of the horse can overwhelm this type of rider. Despite this, the individual still seems to maintain some resemblance of balance due to the way the horse is engulfed or constricted. There is difficulty in using the legs as an aid, because the tendency is to use the trunk of the body and just go along for a ride. This type of rider is often too concerned about "being proper," therefore, the horse becomes spoiled.

. . .

SHRUNKEN
Illustration 4

This rider needs to have a backbone. They must learn to become aggressive and take a stand; if not, the horse takes full advantage with this type of emotional attitude. There is a need or want to be cared for. This rider cannot drive the horse forward because of the collapsed abdomen. The elevation achieved is minimal because of the rider's poor body alignment and a caved-in chest. The horse loves this rider because he can get away with anything. This rider lacks self-confidence to take charge of his mount.

An older, well-trained, horse that is kind and obedient and has small strides can help this type of rider gain self-confidence. Once the rider has enough confidence, he can graduate to a slightly more challenging horse. This is one emotional attitude that benefits greatly from riding horses. The inner strength gained provides the rider with a backbone for strength when facing opposition.

. . .

BALANCE

Nature cares for your balance. It is human nature to seek balance, whether it is physically, mentally or emotionally. This natural process maintains our health and well-being. We simply trust that it is taken care of. In nature, all things have an internal, as well as an external balance.

Balanced riding reconnects the rider to the forces of nature and re-establishes connectivity with heaven and earth energies. Balance is achieved by letting go and allowing the natural forces to uplift and align the rider's position in harmony with that of the horse. The earth provides the stability or receptivity. Heaven provides the vision or experience, meaning, stability and experience, coupled with spontaneity. This combination provides for natural balance. *(Illustration D.)*

Translated, this means riding your horse in balance, allowing spontaneity of action. Spontaneity is developed from experience. One needs practice, and more practice, to develop *Zanchin. (Part One, Communication.)* From this comes the skill to ride in complete harmony, built on stability. More simply put, it means letting go and trusting in nature.

Balance is the fundamental requirement of any physical activity. All movement requires balance for it to be executed. Some have been masters of balance, such as a gymnast or a tight-rope walker. These are extreme examples for the average person, but should be considered in order to become a proficient rider.

Try to balance a book on the top of your head. Proper body alignment and balance is necessary to maintain the position of the book while walking. Taking this further, imagine a backpack filled with schoolbooks. Placing it on your back instantly shifts your center of gravity.

The additional weight upsets your natural balance. If the weight on your back is still, it is easy to maintain your balance. If the weight on your back moves from side to side, balance is disturbed until the weight is fixed in a solid, balanced position.

A horse cannot find his balance if the rider is tossing around in the saddle. The rider must correctly position his body weight and maintain that position. This is accomplished through body awareness, body alignment and balance. Remind yourself to do this each time you ride a horse. A constant reminder will keep you from tossing around in the saddle, or at least to try not to.

• • •

DIRECTION OF ENERGY IN A MISALIGNED RIDER
Illustration C

Poor balance and body alignment of the rider is the determining factor in the direction of energy. A crooked, unbalanced horse, driving on the forehand, reflects the results. The energy becomes forceful and heavy.

A lack of balance forces the rider to balance with the hands. This stops the action, or energy. The horse drops his back and stiffens by locking its jaw and poll to resist this stop action. The under muscle of the neck bulges and the horse begins its movement from its forehand. The rider initiates the energy from the hands and must resort to kicking the horse to urge it forward.

The center of gravity in the rider is thrown forward and the rider grabs with his knees.

The *hara* is sheltered, thus preventing good balance. There is a lack of connectivity with heaven and earth's energy. This does not support an upward-driving motion in balance and with impulsion.

. . .

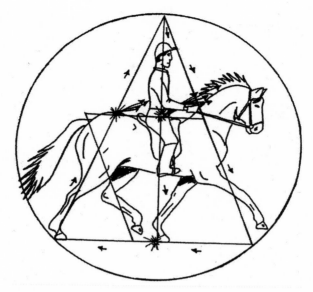

DIRECTION OF ENERGY IN UNITY
Illustration D

First, the rider initiates movement and energy from the *hara*. Leg aids are applied. At that particular moment, energy is sent to the earth. The earth provides the stability and sends the energy to the hindquarters, where it drives the horse upward to meet heaven's energy. Heaven's energy provides the vision or elevation. The two energies meet at the apex of the triangle. Heaven's energy then drives down to meet earth's energy once more, as the cycle repeats itself. The triangle of energy maintains the balance and impulsion. The point where the hands meet the triangle is the union of heaven and earth's forces.

The driving energy from the *hara* climaxes at this point. Combustion takes place. The explosion is directed through the reins, to the bit, and reverts back to the reins, which act as an extension of the arms. From the arms, energy circulates to the *hara* for the recycling process. Horse and rider are aligned with the magnetic forces of heaven and earth. A dynamic exchange of energy takes place.

• • •

CARRYING ENERGY OF HORSE AND RIDER
Illustration E

This demonstrates the forces at work that suspend the horse and rider.

It is the sustaining force of heaven and earth, working to maintain impulsion and elevation.

This force creates and maintains "lightness." It is natural balance.

. . .

Balance originates in the *hara*, or center of gravity. *(Part Four, Breath.)* At this point, the energy of heaven and earth meet to create a gyratory ball of energy. This ball rotates in conjunction with the rotation of the earth. If the earth's gravitational force is altered in any way, our balance will most definitely be affected.

The magnetic poles, which influence the center of the earth's gravity, also influence our center of gravity. *(Illustration B, E and F)* Should they shift, the earth's rotational force would be altered.

This would change the gravitational force and shift our center of gravity.

Let us simplify that. Heaven being the north pole and earth being the south pole, corresponds to our head, which is affected by the north pole, and our feet, which is affected by the south pole. The center is represented by the *hara*. The energy runs directly through the spine. The pull from heaven and earth establishes clarity and balance. The importance of a solid heaven-and-earth connection cannot be underestimated.

For example, to ride a bike, you find your center of gravity or *hara*. With a little practice, you get good at balancing the bike because the *hara* is being developed along with your connectivity to heaven and earth. Once you learn how to ride a bike, you never forget this "feel," or center of balance. Years may pass without ever riding a bike, but you can still get back on the bike and ride without the need to reestablish your balance. Your body naturally picks up where you left off. The brain searches its memory bank for the right "feel" data, enabling your body to remember. *(Part Four, Inner Rhythm and Part One, Communication.)*

Balanced riding requires this same memory. First, correct "feel" is established by learning the rhythm of the horse. Repetition and the help of a good trainer accomplish this. Each time a rider mounts balance is automatically sought. If the rider's weight or center of gravity is slightly forward, this registers in the brain as "feel." The brain tells the rider, "You're off balance." Should the rider lose the connectivity, the horse will have difficulty in lightening the forehand. The energy seems like it is moving forward, but instead, its direction of force is downward into the earth, as opposed to upward toward the heavens. *(Illustration C.)*

It is the rider's responsibility to maintain position within the center of gravity of the horse. This preserves the purity of the gaits. To do this, the horse must be ridden forward and straight. If not, it becomes impossible for the horse to distribute the weight equally on all fours. If the horse is ridden forward and straight, he gains natural balance. *(Illustration E.)*

Natural balance is the foundation of a good seat and symmetrical torso. The seat, including the torso and spine, move with the horse's gaits. The head is balanced on top of the shoulders, not tipped back, forward, or tilted to one side. When the seat is in balance with no undue muscular stiffness, the legs elongate and fall naturally into place. Balance is achieved by suspending with the movement of the horse. It becomes a ballet of harmony between horse and rider. Without a balanced seat, the rider cannot possibly ride the horse forward.

. . .

SELF-CARRIAGE

Three elements comprise self-carriage: body awareness, body alignment, and balance, in successive order. Each degree of awareness is an end to a beginning or a beginning to an end. Similar to stacking blocks, as long as they are stacked equally, one builds upon the other and supports one another. It is a continuous cycle. This is nature's order of things.

A horse in self-carriage is supported by the driving force of the rider's aids. A moment of suspension achieves an effortless, well-balanced, elegant frame. The presentation of the horse becomes dynamic. At that moment, all hard work is paid off. Freedom of expression and unity of two kingdoms, man and animal, is the reward. This is the art of equitation. Self-carriage is demonstrated by lightness, suppleness, forward impulsion, and cadence in every movement.

Self-carriage requires refinement. It doesn't last indefinitely. After moments of self-carriage, the cycle begins again. The energy is circular. There is no beginning and no end. Each beginning climbs one step higher, but the pattern of development remains constant. Simply put, the means to achieve the goal remains the same. The level of refinement or proficiency differs. A plateau of learning is reached, in order to continue, the natural cycle must begin again.

The plateau sometimes is mistaken as the goal. All learning disengages at this point. Recognizing the cycle of learning helps to avoid this common pattern. In most cases, when the rider is challenged with feelings of frustration and inadequacy, a plateau of learning has been reached. A simpler explanation is that of belt ranks in martial arts. The misunderstanding is that reaching black belt is the goal. It is merely the end of one cycle or plateau and the beginning of a new one. Reaching self-carriage indicates the end of one cycle and the beginning of the next.

To refine self-carriage, begin with a conscious awareness of how you stand. For example, standing in line at a bank. Do you stand square and balanced as you ask your horse to do at the halt? Is one hip lower, or is one foot out? Do you recognize anyone in self-carriage? Approaching the teller, do you lean on the counter the same way your horse might lean on your hands? If the rider is not in self-carriage, it is impossible for the horse to be, and unfair to expect this of the horse.

It is common to look for support from objects or another individual. This may be the wall, the counter, the chair, our spouse, friends, and so on. Whoever or whatever it is becomes a crutch. We are not taking full responsibility, even at the simplest tasks.

The next time you stand in line, try to stand square, with your weight equally balanced. It is not easy to do if it has become your habit to lean to one side or the other. When approaching a counter, try not to rest your body weight on it. This, too, takes a certain amount of applied awareness to be successful.

Leaning has become a habit, the same way it has become a habit for your horse to lean on the reins. Perhaps, the rider is the one leaning on the reins for support, and a sympathetic reaction from the horse results. The most important request we ask of the horse is to get off the forehand. Do you think it is possible if the rider continually walks, acts, and thinks on the forehand? By this, I mean walking head first and looking down, unaware of what the body is doing. *(Illustration A.)* You don't need four legs to be on the forehand; our mind puts us there. We all do it, so don't take it so hard. Apply body awareness daily and improve self-carriage within yourself and your horse.

Consistent focused attention allows the habits of the body to change. Focusing attention on the way you carry yourself slowly changes the unconscious habits by making them conscious. You might be surprised to discover how many crutches you have, and how often you shift your body weight from one foot and hip to the other while leaning against the wall.

Another perfect opportunity to practice self-carriage is walking upstairs. If you grab the rail and pull yourself up, you are not practicing self-carriage. This is similar to the horse pulling on the reins, as if the reins will lift his feet up. That would be interesting to see.

Practice bringing your knees up while keeping your body in balance. Both hipbones should be square and supple enough to move up and down, similar to that of your horse. Slowly, take a step upward, with the weight of your body balanced equally on the sole of your foot. The muscles of the buttocks must be engaged to maintain balance. Do not tip forward, but maintain an erect, not stiff, back in balance with the rest of your body. Stay in your center of gravity. Your muscles will object. They are not accustomed to carrying the weight in this manner.

Bring this new awareness of self-carriage into riding. It awakens a new level of communicating with your horse and offers answers to why he refuses to comply with your aids.

A balanced rider keeps his hands silent yet light. The upper body works independently from the lower body while still in unison with each other. Practice walking as a unit. Begin each step from the *hara* and keep the height of the body constant while controlling the amount of swing in the arms. Basically, this means stepping through with your hips while keeping your arms still at your side. This is the same function as the seat in a rising trot and acts to balance the seat and still the hands, encouraging self-carriage. Connecting the segments of the body allows independent use of each unit while still functioning in its entirety, similar to connecting the hindquarters of the horse to the forehand through the topline. Here is where self-carriage begins.

Self-carriage initiates connectivity with the body, mind and spirit. Each is aligned with one another's purpose and works toward achieving the same goal. Focused concentration on the body while stilling the mind initiates control of the body, thus aligning the spirit with the purpose of riding. Refinement of body position leads to self-carriage.

Any art requiring discipline of the mind nurtures self-development and self-carriage. Simple things, such as walking upstairs or standing in line, are training procedures to become a better person. Practice until it becomes second nature. Equestrian art provides the perfect opportunity to practice discipline of the mind by developing focused attention. The body naturally seeks balance and stability. The outcome is self-carriage, an essential ingredient to becoming a proficient rider.

· · ·

RELAXATION AND LETTING GO

Letting go of set beliefs, conditioned habits, attitudes, and thinking patterns relaxes the body and allows the mind to see clearly. Our belief system and attitudes build a self-image that dictates how we view the world. Often, this is a false or distorted view because the self-image is distorted. This is transferred into the art of equitation by restricting the inner vision of the rider, preventing the rider from seeing and experiencing how nature teaches riding. The vision is restricted to only what the rider can perceive. This is within the range of limitations of the mind, imposed by the self-image.

In simpler terms, this means your riding your horse in what you think is "as forward as" the horse can go. The instructor says send him more forward. Your mind says, "He is forward." That is the limitation; instead, accept the instruction and urge the horse forward as directed. This expands the vision of the rider by offering the experience. As the vision expands, the self-image follows. The horse engages its hindquarters; more impulsion and forward movement is experienced. This is recorded in the "feel" library and a vision is automatically received. The mind says, "Aha! I get it." If this happens often enough, eventually, the rider gains clarity, understanding, and an expansion of the overall view or experience. This realization is the first step to relaxation and letting go. The second step is to trust in nature.

Relaxing and letting go changes the pattern of reflexive action and develops trust in nature. Applied to riding, letting go means stop trying to create or manipulate the horse. Applied individually, it means to stop controlling. The outcome is evident. The horse can now utilize the natural gaits with which they are endowed. The rider frees expectations. Instead of creating how the horse should go, the rider learns to "feel" the horse and work within its capabilities and talents. The mind becomes clear, allowing nature to dictate the next move. The natural progression of body awareness, body alignment, balance, self-carriage and focus follows. The pieces of the puzzle fall into place. Each time the rider lets go and relaxes, the results are always positive. A sense of security is the reward. This reassures the rider it is okay to let go.

Trust in nature allows the individual to reclaim his true image instead of trying to live up to a distorted self-image. The rider trusts in nature by allowing the natural movement of the horse to dictate the rhythm and timing of the movement. Nature rewards the rider by positive reinforcement, thus shedding the old image.

Riding induces relaxation and letting go. Riding is a form of moving meditation. Moving meditation is called *dozen*. An activity or movement performed with heightened responsiveness, connectivity and maximum stability is *dozen*. A balanced rider must focus the mind on the rhythm of the horse. The intensity of the focus stills the mind. This controls the will of the mind by allowing freedom, or letting go. Sitting meditation, or Zazen, also accomplishes this same state of alertness.

When the mind lets go, expect to experience an increased awareness and connectivity with the horse and the surrounding environment. At this point, the horse is given the opportunity to move in a supple and relaxed rhythm. The mind stops controlling and lets go.

Relaxation of the body and letting go of the mind is critical to the balanced rider. Any tension held in the rider's body is felt and reflected in the horse. *(Sympathetic Vibration)*. Holding the jaw creates the same reaction in the horse; that is, holding onto the bit instead of it being soft in his mouth. To ask for elevation with a seat that is not supple and supportive results in the horse dropping his back out from under the saddle and trying to grab onto the reins to compensate for the lack of support. The aids are contradictory. The horse does not understand what is being asked.

To try to please the rider, he looks for ways to compensate, because tension in the body and mind of the rider prevents him from responding correctly.

Stored emotional energy and body tension absorbs a large portion of energy, making it unproductive, inhibiting the rider's ability to perform. Practicing proper body alignment alters the muscular structure, triggering a release of trapped emotional energy. Exercise and proper breathing techniques also prompt the release of emotional energy and tension. Relaxation and letting go are natural progressions in self-development. Traditional yoga postures are formulated on this basis to release stored emotions or energy, thus promoting free-flowing *Ki*. *(Part Four, Life Force)*.

Riding alters the muscular structure by aligning the body and elongating the muscles. Letting go encourages the muscle to elongate with less effort. The rider must consider the emotions and attitudes to cultivate relaxation. *(Body Awareness and Body Alignment)*

Stress and anxiety play a role in the body's ability to let go and relax. Unwanted tension is created. Emotions pull from within, and the horse pulls from without. If you feel fear, the horse responds to that fear by worrying. If you are stressed, the horse cannot relax. Your emotional state not only affects those around you, but your horse as well.

Emotions direct the overall pattern of response. This affects the rider's ability to relax and let go. A rider who carries tension in the upper back and scapula perhaps feels as if he carries the weight of the world on his shoulders. During a lesson, the instructor may request the rider to lighten the forehand of the horse. The rider can't because of the tension carried in the neck and shoulders. The fear of letting go determines the response to this request. If the rider can forget himself and let go, lightness is achieved.

Some riders develop more skill than others, and some are more defensive. Emotional energy and feelings are revealed outwardly by a stiff, unyielding body or a supple, open one. This is reflected upon the horse as the rider expresses or inhibits these emotions. *(Illustrations1, 2,3,4)*. The first step to release inner tension is awareness of it. This brings relaxation, and then initiates the process of letting go. The body rebalances and the rider gains more security in the saddle. The need to balance on the reins is lessened. The natural rhythm of the horse is restored.

Deep breathing helps to restore relaxation. Focus on sending the breath to the *hara*. This drops the center of gravity and releases energy after a stressful event. It is common to be relaxed while doing familiar things, and feeling tense and anxious with unfamiliar situations.

Most riders are tense while waiting for the results of a test ride. After the results are known, regardless of the score, relaxation occurs. The anxiety of not knowing no longer exists. The unknown produces tension. An individual always feels more secure in a known and predictable situation.

Maximum physical, mental, and emotional strength comes from performing a physically demanding activity in a relaxed but attentive state of body and mind. At this level of connectivity, inner strength and physical power surges from the *hara*. *(Part Four, Breath)*. The body is relaxed while the mind is alert. This state of relaxation develops stamina while riding. Riding with tension and anxiety is difficult and dangerous.

The simplest of tasks can develop stamina of the body and mind. Have you ever noticed that when you rush while washing the dishes, that is the time when a glass or dish breaks, or you stub your toe or hit your funny bone? More time and energy is expended cleaning up or fixing the mess. It becomes unpleasant and frustrating because, in your efforts to hurry up, more tension was created. This turns into anxiety and nothing is accomplished. It requires stamina of the body and mind to maintain a relaxed body and alert mind.

Clarity of mind and more rational thinking are benefits gained from relaxing and letting go. Relaxation brings an applied awareness to feelings and reactions. Focused attention allows an automatic release that connects the rider with the horse. The mind focuses on the goal and not the negative aspects in between. Focused attention while riding connects the body, mind and spirit. The rider applies body awareness, which then initiates body alignment by causing a shift in muscle tissue. This shift reforms the habits of the body and mind, allowing for synchronicity. The alignment of body, mind and spirit occurs. Take a breath and relax.

One important thing to remember: Do not try so hard. Do not try to create and produce a product or image of what you "think" the horse should be or look like. This is man-made. Let go of the distorted image and allow the horse to be a horse by utilizing its natural gaits. Enhance the beauty of nature by relaxing and letting go. Trust in nature.

· · ·

PART THREE
MIND

. . .

INTRODUCTION

Riding horses is training of the mind. Equestrian art forces the mind to synchronize and focus on the task at hand. The mind must concentrate on body alignment, posture, balance and precise delivery of the correct aids of communication. At the same time, the rider must focus on maintaining the energetic, forward-moving strides of the horse while keeping the tempo or rhythm consistent.

Intense concentration and focus train the mind and activate the use of the entire brain. An effective rider utilizes the feel sense while riding. This engages the right hemisphere or creative, feeling side of the brain. The left hemisphere analyzes what the rider is doing and encourages consistency. Both hemispheres are engaged in the one act of riding. This increases communication and connectivity with the horse and the immediate environment, creating a flexible, movable mind. There is less confrontation with solid communication.

Training the mind builds inner strength, clarity and a sense of security within the environment, while an untrained mind is a wavering, fluctuating mass, with no focus or organization. The results are seen in daily life as success or failure. Training the mind is an asset that cannot be underestimated.

. . .

HUMBLENESS

Riding horses challenges the mind by creating an atmosphere of humility. A humble rider learns from the horse and preserves the naturalness of the gait. The horse mirrors our insecurities. The carriage of the horse not only represents our position, skills, or lack of it, but also is an honest expression of how the rider feels about himself and the world around him. *(Illustrations 1,2,3,4)*. The challenge is in the acceptance of this expression. Humbleness is the key to unlock your greatest potential and that of your horse.

One of the greatest virtues the horse instills is humbleness. He always forgives and allows himself to be humiliated. A horse accepts himself as a horse, and the responsibility that goes with it. He is not trying to change his identity. He graciously obliges us and allows us to sit on his back and ride him. This reflects humbleness.

Humbleness allows us to train him. A rider or trainer who lacks a certain amount of humbleness can inflict unjustified punishments or reprimands on the horse or student. The intention is misdirected because of a self-centered purpose. In many instances, a lack of clarity, focus or individual distortions of self are the cause. This is an egotistical approach and harbors insecurities. The need for control is greater than humbleness and truth. Responsible action is lost. The ego, being self-centered, is concerned only with making an impression. The horse or student is the recipient. Regardless, the horse does not change his image and responsibility. He simply is a horse.

Humbleness, or a lack of it, is revealed in many subtle ways. The relationship between trainer and rider is one example of how humbleness exposes our insecurities. Occasionally, riding instructors are confronted with a new student boasting about his riding skills and at the same time, making an excuse for failure.

What many consider to be riding is actually renting a trail horse for a guided tour, or childhood memories of bouncing around the arena. Despite this, the instructor gives the student the benefit of the doubt and asks for a demonstration. The scenario generally proceeds like this: The rider tries to impress the instructor. What happens is the ego shows off. The instructor, trying to be polite, offers valid corrections. The rider cannot hear what the instructor is saying. The ego is too inflated. Eventually, the instructor has to humiliate the rider to earn respect and be heard. Now, learning takes place.

With the ego in charge, humbleness is rejected. What appears to be abuse and humiliation to the student is constructive analysis. Without humbleness, the ability to accept positive, corrective advice dwindles. Eventually, the rider seeks another trainer. Most likely, this will be one who teaches what the rider wants to hear, not one who teaches them what they need to learn.

A student/trainer relationship can be seen as a bright light revealing the way into self-discovery and harmony with the horse. With the wrong attitude and lack of humility, this light is often insupportable. Simply put, the ego of an individual lacking humbleness is not ready to take responsibility for his actions. The results are expressed outwardly through the horse by a happy, willing-to-work attitude, or a nervous, spooky mount. Without humbleness, the ego of the rider blames the horse or the trainer, and then justifies the blame. This allows the student to quit without feeling like a failure.

At the opposite end, there are many so-called trainers of little competence who force themselves upon the student and wade in self-delusion. It takes a humble student to judge the wisdom of the trainer. It takes a humble instructor to judge the capacity of the student. Choose a trainer wisely. When you find one who teaches what you need, safeguard that relationship like a rare artifact.

Good trainers are ones who possess humility. In humbleness, they continue to learn. They learn from professionals, horses, and their students as well. A good trainer not only instructs, but also is a good listener. This helps the instructor determine if the student understands the lesson.

A humble mind is one of a beginner. The mind of the beginner is fresh and eager to learn. This is where the greatest learning unfolds. The challenge is to maintain that eagerness over time. Riding horses requires work. Not only physically, but mentally and spiritually as well. Humbleness and perseverance can be the virtues to sustain a mind of learning. Realistic expectations help to keep things in perspective.

A lack of humbleness prevents realistic expectations and causes the ego to seek false gratification elsewhere in order to avoid failure. In truth, the ego refuses to take a deeper look inside at the moment of dissatisfaction. Instead, the resistance in the horse is blamed on the horse, instead of the rider checking his position and proper aids of communication. This is the easy way out. Looking outside is safe. Looking inside means having the humbleness to see the truth.

Resentment or anger can also mask the ability to project humbleness. For many, it begins as early as childhood. We are forced into a system that does not cultivate creativity or individuality. We are told how to act, think, and simply be. We tried to fit in for fear of rejection. The outcome was a loss of identity. Humbleness was forced upon us in an unnatural way that weakened us. To avoid rejection, resentment is unconsciously harbored and hidden by insecurities and false identities.

This pattern of resentment manifests in adulthood through our relationships with others and with that of the horse. Healing takes place at a subconscious level while practicing good horsemanship. The horse acts as the catalyst, making it safe to explore those areas of self. Forgiveness reveals the pattern of resentment and allows the search for the "true" self to begin. Discovery happens quickly with humbleness. We walk in darkness without it.

Humbleness leads to emptiness of the mind. There are no expectations. The ability to recognize when you have made a mistake is reinforced with humbleness. Difficulties are overcome. There is no greater virtue than humbleness. Without it, there is no forward movement towards the pursuit of peace, happiness and love.

Progress in the art of equitation requires a humble attitude and love for the horse. This provides an environment of mutual respect and admiration, allowing reciprocity in learning while assisting in our pursuit towards self-discovery.

. . .

TRUTH

My nephew made a comment to me a few years ago. He said, "Auntie, by the time you are forty-five, you will be too old to ride horses." I smiled and said, "Certainly not. I will ride until I am one hundred years old." This pattern of thinking influences the outcome of your life.

Your truth is—what you are willing to accept about yourself. This is a powerful statement. Consider this: If you accept the fact your horse is lazy, then he will be lazy. A simple thought prevents or creates results. The thought becomes your truth. The fact is, you now have an excuse to fail. Excuses hide the truth by manifestations of the defense. This provides the proof that the justification is true or real. A distorted image or illusion of self develops.

I remember being told as a child, "Don't do that, you'll hurt yourself." Well, sure enough, I would hurt myself. Why, because I accepted it as my truth and created it. The "suggestion," which was interpreted as truth, was converted into "a happening." The power of suggestion and its acceptance converts to truth. Without acceptance, it dissipates.

Throughout childhood, capabilities are constantly tested. Fears and doubts fill the mind. These doubts eventually manifest into false truths. Upon maturity, the fears or so-called truths are questioned. Illusion melts and truth is revealed. This is fearful. Until now, full responsibility has been avoided. False securities must be reckoned with. It is easy to admit and recognize that they exist, but do you believe them? The truth is in how you believe in yourself, not what you say about yourself.

What you believe about yourself and your horse determines the outcome of a budding rider and the potential of your horse. If you cannot see the truth in your instructor's words, then how can you possibly make the necessary corrections and benefit from them? You have not accepted it as "your" truth. In your mind, you are already applying the proper aid or body position. You truly believe and accept this, so it is difficult to see otherwise. This is a distorted vision.

If it is an accepted fact that the horse always short strides on his right hind leg, most likely he will. The mind sets up the circumstance to prove this as true. It is up to the individual to change what is believed as the truth. To do this first requires humbleness, and secondly, strength of character.

Humbleness and truth go hand in hand. By this, I mean truth can be viewed clearly and unfiltered if humbleness exists. For example, if your instructor says your shoulder is locked, you must accept it as true. Whether you accept it or not, the horse will show you. Your state of body and mind is reflected outward through the movement of your horse.

This is how the horse teaches us the truth. It becomes so evident that we cannot deny it. Why would you want to? Avoiding the truth defeats the purpose of one's efforts to improve. Use riding as a spiritual tool to bring clarity into the illusion of self. Riding is such that anyone who chooses to perfect equestrian art cannot help but gain clarity and learn to take responsibility for their actions.

· · ·

RESPONSIBILITY = SUCCESS

A lack of responsible action takes away personal power and prevents success. Most of the time, the power is given to the doctor, attorney, teacher, parent, spouse, or friends. Whenever something goes wrong, the blame is put on some outside influence, and then given to someone else to correct it. Doing this stunts spiritual growth.

Denying responsibility prevents the rider from utilizing sympathetic vibration and improving. It is much easier to blame the horse for the faulty carriage or blame the instructor for poor communication. A responsible rider improves. Improvement leads to success. Evasions from the horse, such as running to the gate, come to an end. The rider takes responsibility for the circumstance. Confidence is gained through success. This changes the individual outlook in daily life. Taking responsibility means realizing the only circumstance in life is self-created.

Conditions are subconsciously formed to allow us the opportunity for personal growth and responsibility. Sadly enough, the majority of the time, the mind justifies the outcome of the circumstance with an explanation or excuse. This becomes the normal pattern of doing things. In actuality, the explanation hides the guilt and the mind replaces the failure with blame instead of taking responsibility for the incident. This creates an attitude of acceptance that allows the excuse or explanation. In this way, responsibility can be rejected without shame or guilt.

Suppose you are cantering in an area of the arena where you know there are some rocks and the footing is uneven. Your horse steps on a rock, twisting his leg and injuring a ligament. Now, he is lame. Who is at fault here? Many may try to hide their guilt by holding the proprietor responsible for the rocks and uneven footing in the arena. To a certain point, yes, he is responsible; but who told you to ride there? With guilt, there is always a deep feeling of dissatisfaction because your heart knows where the responsibility lies.

Explanations or denial of the truth may prevent an embarrassing moment, but they do not promote spiritual growth. Failure is justified by the explanation and is supported by an illusion of truth. If the support or illusion crumbles, your world is shaken up or falls apart. Statements such as, "I can't;" "I'm too old;" "My horse is moody;" or, "I'm not flexible," are only justifications for failure. For every excuse that is perceived as truth, it gains power and is deeply embedded in the subconscious.

This is the beginning of a habit. The habit is refusal to take responsibility for one's actions in all aspects of life. Regardless of the number of riding lessons, progress is made only by taking personal responsibility for correct body position and alignment. The rider who slouches throughout the day will never be correctly positioned in the saddle until full responsibility is taken and excuses are non-existent. Blame is replaced with responsibility and success is the result.

Riding is a responsibility to yourself and to the comfort of your horse. Owning a horse or any animal is a responsibility that requires commitment. Taking responsibility in life requires a commitment to yourself. If there is no commitment, there is no responsibility. For many, it is safer that way. For instance, an individual who purchases horses as the finishing touch to their architectural dream. This is a self-centered purpose and there is a lack of commitment to the well-being of the horses. It is purely for aesthetics and the inflated ego enjoys bragging to the socialites about the progress they are making. The horse is discarded if it no longer meets the standards of the ego. Responsibility in this case is discarded as well.

Responsibility means facing the truth. The truth is, one cannot live up to the social expectations of a distorted self-image. The motivation is for the wrong reasons. In reality, it is an illusion. Fear of success or of discovering one's true identity is the underlying evil in this vicious circle. Fear of success does not allow commitment and responsibility. Success forces one to see the truth. It means changes must be made. The mind is not always willing to accept the responsibility involved with change.

This means admitting that your shoulder was locked and the lateral movement was a forced movement, not a natural one, or that maybe, you are responsible for your horse's laziness. This is the challenge. It is easier to put the blame elsewhere.

Hundreds of years ago, in the native Indian tribes, children were given responsibilities that were not burdens but rites of passage. The old ones would take the children out and pass on knowledge to them about the fruits, nuts, berries, and vegetables. When the children learned it well, they would go out with tribal members and gather food. Soon, the children were entrusted with the responsibility of teaching other young ones. A mistake could perhaps cost the life of themselves and others. They learned the value of responsibility quickly. The consequences have changed, but the value and commitment remain the same.

To regain personal power is to take responsibility for one's successes and failures. Success means taking responsibility and facing the consequences, whether good or bad. To take responsibility means taking an honest look at yourself. Responsibility initiates self-evaluation, thus cultivating personal growth.

. . .

SELF-EVALUATION

The path to self-improvement and spiritual growth is to have constant evaluation. Seek the truth and apply what we know as truth in every action. To do this requires evaluation of our actions. An honest and sincere look at the true intentions for an action eventually leads to an awareness of the habit requiring change, thus initiating the improvement. Evaluations are the tool that leads to self-mastery and development of an art.

Personal growth and spiritual evolution cannot be achieved with a mind that denies responsibility and change. There must be a strong desire to recognize and then reject illusion or self-created truths. This entails analyzing your intentions and reactions, then applying them for the benefit of others. Without self-evaluation, an individual is drawn to the path of moral deprivation.

The horse cannot be expected to improve its gait if there is no examination and evaluation of the training of the horse. In an honest evaluation, growth occurs. First, an acknowledgment must be made that improvement is needed, and then change begins.

Most riders are quick to punish the horse for not executing a balanced stride. If honest evaluation is employed, the rider always looks inward first before putting the blame elsewhere. This practice constantly creates an environment for self-mastery.

Self-evaluation is a test of inner strength. All boundaries are pushed to their limits, and then some. Only the strong survive such honest evaluations and still come out untarnished. The ability to go beyond the limitations of the mind reflects outward as unity between horse and rider. Honest evaluation eventually grows to emanate perfection. The most effective form of training the body and the mind is the self-initiated effort of self-evaluation.

. . .

COMMITMENT, DISCIPLINE, AND REPETITION

A student of martial arts has inexhaustible discipline and commitment to withstand the rigors of training. The professional athlete and the successful executive have three things in common: commitment, discipline, and repetition. Throughout history, major achievements and advancements have been made using this formula.

The prerequisite for the art of equitation requires this same formula, with no exceptions. Halfhearted commitment brings on laziness and accidents occur with a lack of discipline. The horse cannot have discipline if the trainer is not disciplined. A weak character cannot possibly handle a horse with a strong temperament. The discipline is self-driven and requires a commitment to yourself and the horse. It is an expression of your veracity.

Commitment and discipline create change. If an individual applies discipline to follow through with a commitment, such as equestrian art, trust in one's self is the end result. Trust leads to more discipline. Each builds upon the other for strength and stability of character. For discipline to be effective, it first requires commitment, followed by repetition. A basic example is your commitment to learn balanced riding. This initiates a search for an instructor.

After finding the right instructor for your level of commitment, you then disciplined yourself to take riding lessons once a week. The weekly lesson provides the repetition that leads to the goal of balanced riding.

Commitment provides the necessary frame of mind for discipline. Discipline brings improvement in the attitude and control of the mind. Repetition is the skill that retrains the body and mind. Without commitment, there is no discipline to provide the motivation for repeated practice or repetition.

Different levels of commitment determine your level of success. A commitment made halfheartedly produces halfhearted results. It is easy to be fooled into believing that you gave it your best shot. Are you being honest with yourself? Did you commit one hundred percent effort to achieve maximum results? In your heart, the truth lies.

The amount of commitment is reflected by the outcome. Your horse will be balanced and straight, or crooked and on the forehand. The denial of failure keeps the individual from admitting a lack of absolute commitment. An example might be something as simple as picking out the debris from the horse's hooves. The horse may show resistance in lifting his left hind foot. Therefore, someone else is asked to do it, or it is left alone. Perhaps, every time the horse is being bridled, he throws his head up, making it hard to reach. To solve this, a stool is used. The mind convinces the self that it is not a problem and prevents clear translation of the intention of the horse. The commitment was not made to overcome this small inconvenience and teach the horse proper manners. It is much easier to disregard it or work around it.

The mind chooses to avoid confrontation and justifies it by allowing excuses for failure. The excuse says it is okay to accept this type of behavior. This is not commitment. This is an excuse for lack of commitment and therefore, lack of success.

If you decide to lose weight, the way to success is to make a commitment, then to discipline your eating habits by applying repetition. This reestablishes new guidelines for eating. Perhaps, add an exercise program to the schedule also. This produces long-lasting results. A lack of commitment produces short-term weight loss. Within a few months, the pounds are back because discipline was replaced with an excuse. A common excuse is, "I'm doing good, one bite of that cake won't hurt me." Repetition to create new eating patterns is prevented by the excuse.

Doing things only when you want to does not produce results. Reasons such as, "I'm too tired, I'll do it later, and it doesn't seem to be working" are common justifications for not succeeding. It requires commitment, discipline, and repetition to achieve permanent and rewarding success.

Look at your successes and failures. Your achievements reflect a commitment that you made to yourself. It took a certain amount of discipline and repetition for the commitment to develop into success. Failures need to be looked upon honestly, with an open heart, to admit a halfhearted commitment.

Granted, not everyone has the same potential. How do you know your potential without applying one hundred percent effort? Commitment, discipline and repetition turns on a faucet of wealth and knowledge into the divine aspects of the human soul.

The horse demands your commitment. It comes from the heart, with a sincere desire to provide quality care for the horse. Discipline then becomes effortless and joyful. Repetition is painless and mindful. This formula: commitment, discipline, and repetition, brings new gains: self-confidence, self-respect, and trust.

. . .

SELF-CONFIDENCE

Self-confidence nurtures strong communication and a good relationship with your horse. A self-confident rider with skill can easily get a horse to respond to their commands. A simple habit, such as a horse that pulls on the lead rope, grabbing at the blades of grass along the way, can either be reinforced by a casual rider or corrected by a self-confident rider who applies commitment, repetition and discipline. If the ill behavior is not corrected, it develops into a habit, and the horse takes full advantage. Soon, it becomes difficult to lead the horse.

A rider lacking self-confidence is set up for failure. The horse sets them up. Balanced riding builds confidence. A horse gains confidence and trust from a self-confident rider. The horse takes advantage of a rider who lacks confidence.

A poorly trained horse can learn confidence from an experienced and confident rider or trainer. For example, forcing a horse into executing a movement in which he does not have the stamina or talent causes failure. The horse loses confidence in his own ability and that of the rider. Every time he is asked for the same movement, he fails because he remembers a bad experience. Proper re-schooling with someone he trusts rebuilds confidence in the horse. The horse no longer feels the need to run from the bad memory because he is confident in the trainer. The rewards of this are experienced through better communication and a relationship built on trust.

. . .

TRUST

Trust is an unspoken, understood power. It is silently accepted and felt as something commanding and sacred. It challenges you mentally and emotionally, yet it nurtures and offers a sense of security or knowingness. The essence of your relationship with your horse is built on trust. This establishes the foundation that bonds and nurtures the training of the horse. For the horse to trust you, you must trust yourself. This means not only trusting in your abilities, but also in the silent messages received, such as a "feeling" that something is not right. The natural response to this feeling is to distrust because of logic. We are taught to believe and trust only that which is tangible. This is an area where the horse is a good teacher.

Horses trust in nature. They do not live separate from the source of life, as we tend to do. All animals in the wild maintain this level of trust to survive. This connectivity to nature can be recognized by the animals' change of behavior, sometimes, days before an approaching storm is seen. When a natural disaster is about to strike, have you noticed how all wildlife seems to disappear? There is a haunting silence in the air. Ancient tribes used this instinct, too. They lived in tune with the earth. They trusted the messages of the earth. The domesticated horse has retained this natural instinct and is given a new challenge of trust—humans.

Domesticating horses or any animal creates a dependency or reliance that is based on trust. The horse no longer has to search for food or be on the look out for predators; instead, he entrusts his well-being to us. A horse that suddenly shies at the corner of the arena is less apt to run out of control if the horse trusts the rider. With an inexperienced rider and an untrusting horse, this can be a dangerous and frightening experience.

Trust translates to obedience in the horse. It feels secure, knowing the rider will not endanger it nor ask it to execute a movement beyond its capability. With advancement, trust becomes mutual. Each time you are able to execute a beautiful, forward-moving trot, you trust your abilities, and the horse trusts you. This is how the horse teaches trust.

Accomplishments develop self-confidence and trust. Achievements provide the incentive to never give up. As trust develops, more is accomplished. Perhaps, you can get your horse to execute two strides of a leg yield without a struggle. What a thrill. This is an incentive built on trust. Contentment with yourself and your horse is the result. It is self-knowing. Trusting yourself leads to self-respect, an essential ingredient that allows trust to flourish. Self-respect is earned and negligence ceases. The attitude becomes one of caring. Only when you develop a profound understanding of trust can you rise above the limitations of the mind.

. . .

SELF-RESPECT

Abuse lies in a lack of self-respect, and many times, animals are the recipients. Without self-respect, unconscious behavior dictates the form of abuse. This does not necessarily mean violent treatment. It is as simple as taking the horse out of the stall, where he has been for the past week, hopping on, and expecting a good ride even without any warm-up procedures. Is it any wonder that, the next day, the horse is lame or uncooperative? The horse was not respected and prepared properly for the vigorous activities.

Would you jump out of bed and immediately run a marathon? Let's hope not. There is an unconscious level of self-respect for your body that tells you so. You respect your body and prepare it properly, otherwise, injuries or discomfort are the result.

Self-respect and suffering are interrelated. Where there is a lack of self-respect, there is suffering. The suffering can take on many subtle forms, such as laziness or greed. This selfish behavior is inflicted on the nearest subject, in this case, the horse, leading to abuse. Lame horses are ridden, improper tack is used, and saddle pads are left dirty. This demonstrates a lack of self-respect and the horse is the one that suffers. Would you wear shoes that hurt your feet or clothes that reek of perspiration? An activity such as riding horses allows this subtle abuse.

The horse is a good target because of its size and willingness to please, contributing to unconscious abuse and a lack of self-respect. There is false gratification derived from gaining control over such a large animal. It gives personal power to the individual ego. The drawback is, without self-respect, this personal power hides weakness of character. If the individual does not face their own weakness, they do not have to change. Instead, the ego continues to create situations to gain more power.

The ego is like an inflated balloon. If you inflate the balloon beyond its normal boundaries of elasticity, it will pop. When the ego becomes inflated beyond its limitations, it will burst. The truth is revealed and there is no longer a facade in which to hide. For many, this becomes a vicious cycle. To face a weakness is fearful because the ego has to recognize that it is not flawless. It means change. Instead, the cycle begins over again.

Self-respect develops an appreciation for life. It begins with appreciating yourself better. Give your body the respect it deserves. Eat food that nourishes, not deprives the body. Get proper exercise and abstain from a lifestyle that does not contribute to your well-being.

Self-respect can make life elegant. Wearing second-hand clothes with dignity is easy if you have self-respect. Throwing clothes on the floor and leaving dirty dishes lying around reflect a poor mental attitude and a lack of self-respect. Good habits and a positive outlook are the results of self-respect.

All living creatures deserve the same respect you give to yourself. Elevate your consciousness to the point of having too much self-respect to ever allow your horse to wear ill-fitted clothes, just the same as not allowing yourself to wear them. Self-respect is earned by trustworthiness and a sense of pride. It is the attitude that says, "I deserve the best." Self-respect turns into compassion for those less capable than yourself.

· · ·

COMPASSION

Self-respect initiates compassion. What is gained by self-respect develops the ability to be sympathetic. This does not mean feeling sorry for someone. By contrast, it is the opposite. You feel what they feel. You do not delve into their sorrow or pain, but become compassionate of it. Compassion equips an individual to console instead of to ridicule.

A simple thought of happiness transforms sadness to joy. Immediately, a smile appears on your face. This is contagious. Perhaps, the recipient was having personal problems. You just initiated a transformation. This is compassion; the capacity and willingness to remove suffering from others and replace it with love.

There is an innate connectivity with all life in each one of us. During anger and rage, compassion is lost and there is a moment of separation. Afterwards, there may be feelings of regret. Many times, unjust treatment is met with a complete reversal as soon as compassion surfaces. An example might be an enraged mother who strikes a child. After the rage settles, the mother feels remorse and tries to amend her wrong actions. Connectivity is re-established. This is where compassion lives.

You may have experienced an episode of anger while riding. You just cannot seem to get your horse to respond. In anger, he is reprimanded. As you settle down and realize it was not his fault, you feel regret. Compassion resurfaces with a guilty conscience.

Compassion is at the seat of connectivity with the source of life. Consider riding your horse with compassion. You will ride with fair treatment. This can be as simple as allowing the horse to take a breather and walk after executing a strenuous movement. Riding with compassion does not permit such things as saddle sores or dirty pads. The benefit gained is a deeper level of communication with the horse. The horse trusts and respects you. Heightened awareness of the efforts of the horse is cultivated, as well as honest evaluation of his potential. Your heart is filled with love and understanding. More compassion means less suffering.

• • •

COMPROMISE

If you have ever had the opportunity to watch a spider weave its web, you learn that, in nature, there can be no compromise. The intricacy involved to create this masterpiece can mean the difference between a full or empty stomach for that spider. If the spider was to compromise and get lazy about building this web, the price to pay can be grand.

If vision is compromised, so too, is reality. The mind creates a vision of what you see as perfection. It is the quality of this vision that creates your reality. It becomes your truth. For example: If your horse executes a leg yield by lazily dragging the hindquarters and barely crossing the front legs, the vision is compromised because you have accepted less than perfection. If you ask the horse to execute a movement and he does not give one hundred percent, you have compromised by accepting partial results.

This does not infer asking a less talented horse to perform like an Olympic athlete. What it does imply is to ask for perfection within the skill level of the horse. Do not compromise your skills or the horse's potential by settling for halfhearted effort and performance.

The horse only gives what you expect. If you expect the horse to fail, then he will. If you expect a perfect leg yield, you will have one. Before expecting one hundred percent effort from the horse, the mind must have a vision of the goal.

Along with vision, the rider needs absolute confidence. This eliminates doubt and allows the goal to be achieved by intention. If the rider does not have a vision of the goal, it is impossible to reach the goal. Take it upon yourself to be exposed to the best in your field. It does not matter what type of riding; what is important is to create a vision of the goal. Once the vision is implanted, the next step is to execute it. It takes work.

A mind that is lazy and offers excuses cannot possibly expect to walk away with the blue ribbon. You get out of the horse what you expect from it. If compromise is what you choose, compromise is what you will have.

Doubt is a contributing factor in compromise. The mind may doubt your ability to execute a proper movement. Because of this, the clouds of doubt move in to blur vision. Doubt is like a rainy day; things become difficult to see and do. The horse receives doubt from the rider and is confused. At this point, the horse executes a resemblance of what was asked. The horse gave its best efforts. Doubt clouded the avenue of communication. The results are compromised. The mind says, "See, I knew we couldn't do it." This confirms your doubt.

The simple rain cloud just grew into a storm. Sometimes, a storm may take days to pass. Have you ever noticed that after a storm, the world around you seems clearer? When doubt lifts, so does compromise. You regain sight of the vision or goal.

It takes determination and focused effort to not compromise and settle for a lazy execution. On occasion, the horse becomes lazy and says in many ways, "I don't want to do this today." In this case, a compromise ingrains the habit of laziness. If the horse realizes he does not have to give one hundred percent effort, he has the advantage.

Concentrated intent or focus should be utilized to correct undesirable actions. If the rider is not precise and strongly focused, a battle of wills begins. If the horse wins, the compromise is remembered. This means that tomorrow, the problem will be amplified. Why should the horse work hard if previously, little effort was acceptable? This can mount into a difficult battle with a stubborn horse that feels he has given enough. Always strive for full execution within the range of ability of the horse. This eliminates the opportunity for the horse to develop undesirable habits. Do not compromise the dignity of the horse.

This applies to simple groundwork also. If a horse refuses to step into or over a puddle in front of the wash rack and you compromise by accepting this action, it is reinforced. Soon, it becomes difficult to approach the wash rack.

The horse learns it is acceptable to refuse. He uses this to his advantage. He becomes a bully every time he is faced with this situation. This carries over into other areas. This situation could have been prevented if the handler did not compromise. This acceptance is a compromise of manners.

Suppose an inexperienced rider takes a horse out and lunges it. The horse acts up and scares the rider. The rider immediately puts the horse away. Can you imagine the difficult pattern that develops? Allowed to continue, it becomes impossible for the horse to be lunged. The horse learns that he gets rewarded for acting in an unruly manner. The negative behavior is reinforced, compromising the talent, manners and dignity of the horse. This can be dangerous. Experience and skill build confidence, so compromise is not acceptable.

Compromise begins in the mind. Do not compromise your values or the elegance of the horse because of a lazy body and mind. It is easy for the mind to convince the body it is tired. This nurtures compromise. Condition the body and mind by commitment, discipline and repetition. By doing so, compromise is not a consideration. The horse becomes an example of elegance. There is dignity even in the smallest of things. To compromise means to sacrifice truth.

. . .

ORDERLINESS

Thoughts require organization. Organization prepares the thoughts for action. This creates orderliness. Goals are first outlined, and steps are arranged. This initiates action towards achievement of the goal. If one step is taken before the other, failure is inevitable. Preparation before a sequence of events can occur is crucial. Before preparation comes orderliness. A good example is cooking. First, the mind becomes orderly by clarifying exactly what you want to cook. Next, the ingredients are collected. At last, the actual preparation takes place. At this point, a sequence of steps begins to initiate achievement. The final goal: you have dinner. Orderliness of the mind is the catalyst that initiates the preparation and sequence of events.

Cooking dinner is not much different from training a horse. It requires orderliness. If you want a vegetable casserole for dinner but skip the preparation, obviously, the result will not be a vegetable casserole. If you want your horse to execute a proper flying change but forget the essential prep work, you have a crooked, unbalanced horse that barely gets off the ground. Most likely, he will trip as his legs get tangled because he has not developed the coordination or muscular strength to execute the movement. He tries to please his rider, yet is punished for his efforts. No horse deserves this treatment. Develop an orderly and consistent training schedule. Consider the ability of you and your horse. Disappointment comes from disorderly training.

Orderly training begins with orderliness of the mind. Regardless of the riding discipline, think about the goal. Then prepare by applying orderliness, collecting the ingredients that initiate the goal. Keep each step, building strength from the previous one. This enables a better overview of the end results for each particular training session. From there, the rate of training progresses according to the ability of the horse and rider. Everything remains in its natural succession, and is orderly.

The need to rush the training of the horse for one's own satisfaction inevitably leads to destruction. Inconsistent and disorderly training habits are hazardous to your physical, mental and spiritual health, and that of your horse.

Preparation and orderliness before riding is just as important as during riding. The rider should prepare by stretching the muscles, adjust the posture, adjust the breath, and empty the mind. This preparation begins an orderly training session. Before all exercise, there should be a warm-up period. It is the natural order of things.

Sadly enough, this step is often neglected. Warm-up prepares the rider and the horse. Both benefit. Physically, the horse is more flexible and less prone to injury. Mentally, the horse is ready to work. Spiritually, the horse enjoys the work.

Preparation prepares a stiff, tense rider by relaxing the body, easing the mind, and developing a feeling of trust. Let us assume you had a stressful day. You arrive at the stables, full of tension and knots. Your body aches. Your mind is filled with chatter. Your breath is short, and your mood is grumpy. What do you think will happen to your horse if you were to ride it while feeling this way?

Your horse reflects your mood and stiffness. It guarantees confrontation with your horse. He does not like your grumpy mood. Being grumpy gives you permission to put aside compassion. Warm up your body, mind and spirit for your horse's sake. You will be glad you did. If you are prepared physically, mentally and emotionally, the results speak for themselves.

Orderliness of the mind is not something to partake of only when riding. A strong character develops orderliness in everything they do. For example: Is your car clean and orderly? How about your home or work environment? Be honest with yourself.

Cluttered rooms and cars filled with litter represent a mind filled with confusion and clutter. Take a look at what is going on in and around you. It reflects the state of mind within. It represents your vision or reality. The need to possess old emotions, hurts, and thoughts become cobwebs in the closets of the mind. Spring-cleaning is recommended throughout the year to rid the mind of unnecessary litter. Wipe those cobwebs off the walls. Shed light into the darkest corners. This allows for expansion and development of the mind and spirit. The body becomes happier, and healthier also. The extra burdens are lifted. The mind cleanses the body.

Are your closets overflowing? Is there an insecurity hanging on the door of your mind, refusing to let go? Evaluate all things in their right perspective and gain clarity. This gives your mind an orderly approach to achieving success. If other aspects of your life are in confusion, how can you ride and expect results afterward?

An orderly mind recognizes a solution to every possible problem because of clarity. If you look through a dirty windshield while driving, things look clouded and dull. Clean the windshield and a new light shines in on your environment. Polish your riding skills with an orderly mind, and you polish the windows of the mind as well.

. . .

CONCENTRATION AND FOCUS

Concentration is commonly understood to mean focusing the mind on one fixed point. Concentration and focus practiced while riding is the dispersion of awareness, so that concentration is moving, not fixed and the focus is direct and precise. Involvement with the surrounding environment is complete while not losing awareness of a single object.

What this means is, the rider's mind is not fixed on the evasions of the horse. Instead, the mind is focused and concentrated on the goal. By doing this, the mind remains flexible and can quickly adjust the position of the rider. This allows the rider to remain in contact with the horse, or to join forces. They are in "sync" with one another's purpose. At this point, connectivity with the surrounding environment is aroused. All action is initiated by feel. Total concentration and focus leads to immersion. To synchronize with your horse, you must be totally immersed with him. Distractions no longer exist.

A simple example is listening to music. Everyone listens to music. If your favorite song is playing, you "zone" into the music. If you are by yourself or in your car with the windows up, you may sing with the tune. It doesn't matter how loud or what it sounds like, because there is no self-consciousness. You are concentrating on the music. Your focus is on the rhythm of the music. You become absorbed with the tune. A knock at the door or a honk at the traffic light startles you. You now are self-conscious. You wonder if someone heard you or noticed what you were doing.

To become a proficient rider, a level of concentration that loses the self and gains "synchronicity" is the goal. Intention is applied and focused, communication is clear and precise and the rider's body, mind and spirit are totally engaged in the performance. You are in the "zone." *(Part Three, No Mind)*. At this point, the simple act of making eye contact with a spectator diverts engagement of the entire self and breaks the level of intensity. The individual becomes self-conscious and loses the synchronicity.

Self-consciousness is subservient to concentration. To gain the ability of body, mind and spirit unification, the mind cannot be inflexible. It must have the ability to move freely while remaining focused and concentrating. A moving, concentrated mind focuses on the purpose or goal while maintaining awareness of the surrounding environment. In other words, there is no "you" involved. There is no concern whether someone is watching. Instead there is total immersion or engagement in the performance. Have you noticed that when you try to show off, that's the time when you make the most mistakes? Your horse probably does something ridiculous, such as tossing his head or deciding to urinate as you halt at X. Concentration and focus were displaced. Self-consciousness took over. Instead of concentrating on leg aids and balance, your mind said, "Look at me. Don't I look great?" or "I hope no one saw that," in an embarrassing moment. To conquer self-consciousness requires conditioning of the mind.

To strengthen the mind, practice daily by controlling the chatter of the mind. Insist the mind concentrate and focus on the object of intention when you ask. Make everything you do an effort towards conditioning the mind. Do not allow excuses to take charge. All that is needed is one hundred percent concentration and focus, even on the simplest of tasks. While cleaning the stall, where is your mind? Keep it focused on the present moment. This conditions the mind to remain still and eliminate unwanted thoughts and feelings. While riding, it gives a head start.

Concentration must have focus. First, you learn to concentrate and become immersed. You then focus or direct your intention to achieve results. A beginner learns to concentrate on their seat. With enough concentration and practice, intention is focused and balance is developed. Concentration creates the catalyst, allowing focus to be applied and results manifested.

The advanced rider expands concentration. Instead of focusing on one part, the focus is on the entire process. Concentration is applied in totality. Intention is focused to create "synchronicity" of horse and rider. The amount of concentration and the intensity of focus determine the amount of "synchronicity." This is important. Concentration without focus is like "zoning" out, rather than "zoning" in.

It is obvious a beginner does not have the intensity of concentration and focus as an Olympian does. It should be equally obvious that a young horse does not have the amount of concentration as a mature, experienced one. Asking a young horse to maintain a high level of concentration for an extended period of time is like asking a two-year-old child to sit still and read a book.

Successful training recognizes the importance of concentration. The trainer who asks too much concentration from the two-year-old filly becomes frustrated when the horse does not comply. It learns as it matures. Quality concentration is worth more than hours of unproductive effort.

The horse's level of concentration increases according to the level of concentration the rider has. A mature horse can lack concentration if the rider lacks the concept of it. Practice and determination increase a rider's concentration and focus with intensity and stability. Proper schooling and focused intentions increase the horse's concentration with intensity and stability.

Involvement in any physical activity requiring concentrated effort and focus brings inner strength and calmness of character. Total engagement triggers concentration and focus, cleansing the body, mind and spirit. A spiritual bath purifies the mind of negativity and rejuvenates the body. This is accomplished by concentration and focus. Riding provides the opportunity to wash away the chatter of the mind.

A moment of "synchronicity" with your horse brings joy and contentment. In that instant, the mind is empty. It is refreshing; the whole world is a pleasant place to be. Total immersion brings us present-moment happiness. Concentration and focus initiate purification of the body, mind, and spirit leading to *mushin*.

· · ·

NO MIND

Mushin or no-mind is a state of total awareness or attentiveness. It is one step beyond concentration to a place where action becomes instinctual. It is interrelated with "effortless effort." *(Next Chapter)*. Each compliments the other. To achieve "effortless effort," a state of *mushin* is necessary, and in order to cultivate no-mind, effortless effort is simultaneously employed.

Mushin can be referred to as "the zone." All of the senses are alive and active yet the mind is void of thought. Actions are initiated from a place of instinct or knowingness that is influenced not by thought but by the rhythm of the internal and external *ki. (Part Four, Life Force)*. The body, mind and spirit are totally engaged in the activity. Every move of the horse or of another individual is predictable *(Zanchin)*.

At this level of intensity, a thought is a distraction and displaces the concentration and focus allowing the internal and external *ki* to be dispersed. More simply put, a distraction allowed to manifest breaks the synchronicity of the activity. Developing the mind to this degree of readiness or alertness can mean the difference between a life of harmony or one of chaos.

For the rider, it means success or failure in cultivating your potential and that of the horse. It is the difference between riding for pleasure and the art of equitation. To further explain this, let's go for a ride. It's been a hard day at work. You arrive at the barn, groom and tack your horse, and proceed to the arena. Leaving the day's stress behind, you ride by simply trusting in your skills, knowledge and instinct.

The ride is exhilarating. The horse is fully attentive to your aids and is executing movements never thought possible. You are in "the zone" and experiencing *mushin*. This was so rewarding that you want to duplicate it one more time. Your efforts fail because at the point of realization, thoughts entered the mind and tried to recreate the moment by controlling it. The thought stopped the action.

To achieve *mushin*, trust in your skills and ride without a doubt. Step into "the zone" by becoming instinctive or by banishing conscious thought. Just perform. Do what you have practiced repetitively. The technical skill is there now; apply it. Application of skill and knowledge applied with a mind of *mushin* is a determining factor in developing your potential as a rider.

With the experience of no-mind comes "lightness." "Lightness" is the carrying power of the horse. *(Part Two, Body Awareness)*. In the "zone," you are aware of the body and controlling it, yet feel as light as a feather and effortless in motion. The lighter your body gets, the more elevation and forward impulsion from the horse is achieved. It drives the horse. It is uplifting.

The experience of "lightness" is stored in the "feel" library. This memory instinctively is sought with each ride. It is like searching a library for the right book. Focusing on the "feel" of lightness locates it in the "feel" library, and attainment of *mushin* is possible. To reach this point requires a disciplined body and mind, along with the correct technical skills to excel.

Mushin requires hours of practice and devotion. First, the basics are learned: a balanced seat, correct leg aids, and proper use of the hands. Practiced consistently, it becomes second nature, like driving a car. You don't need to think about how to drive the car; you just drive it.

Proficient skills and repetition are the links to connecting with the zone. This allows the mind to remain empty, contributing to the level of performance. The introduction of the thought of a technique hinders the rider because the mind stops to think how to apply the leg aid instead of just applying it from instinct.

Watch an Olympic dressage rider. The performance does not look like a particular technique or procedure. Instead it is a manifestation of the skills and procedures practiced and ridden by instinct. It comes together in its entirety and appears to be an

outstanding display of talent. The spectator never sees the hard
work that went into that performance, only the result of that work.
Perseverance, practice and devotion produced the result.

Mushin extends your range of knowingness and focus. A
profound understanding of nature is discovered. The mind is not
distracted by environmental stimulus. The ability to see and
evaluate the present situation is viewed from a place of detachment.
Detachment brings clarity. What this means is becoming detached
emotionally from the horse. Doing so produces clarity. You are
able to see and sense the intentions of the horse without getting
emotionally involved with it.

A simple example might be this: You are riding in the same
arena you normally do. There is one area of the arena where your
horse likes to spook. He uses this to his advantage. A few seconds
before approaching this spot, your mind stops and says, "I'm afraid
he is going to spook." The first thing that happens is the mind
thinks it. This thought brings tensions in the body and creates the
response in the horse. Fear, being added, complicates the situation.
This brings an emotional response, making it difficult to see the
way out. Panic sets in. The horse spooks. Control of the horse is
lost. The horse has the advantage. He remembers it and uses it at
his discretion.

To change this situation, the rider remains detached. This is
accomplished by controlling the mind. If there is no thought,
there is no emotion. Disregard and ignore that he "always" does it.
Simply ride past the same spot, without thinking about it. Treat it
as any other place in the arena. This does not mean a lack of
awareness or preparedness.

Detachment allows instant rectification. Composure and
control are maintained. Ride through the problem area as if it
were not a problem. Awareness of the possibility that the horse
may spook allows for "right" action. The mind is not stuck or
obsessed with the thought of what the horse might do. Since the
horse no longer has the advantage, he eventually decides it is not
worth his efforts.

A mind void of thought or judgment and emotionally detached from a situation maintains a state of *mushin*. The mind is strengthened; awareness expands and reaction time increases. The benefit gained from a state of *mushin* is every movement becomes effortless. You become the master of your mind, instead of the other way around.

. . .

EFFORTLESS EFFORT

The horse has more physical power than we have. Force used against power will not preserve the elegance of the horse and does not produce constructive results. In Xenophon's book on horsemanship, written over two thousand years ago, he observed that forceful training of the horse could never result in cooperation. Throughout history, this concept remains, yet is still misunderstood in relation to the training of the modern horse.

The setback originates in the mind of the rider. Training the mind cannot be underestimated. The rider learns to control the limitations of the mind and becomes a channel of creativity. Expression is created by freedom, not by force, and by trust, instead of by control. A rider trying too hard to "make it happen" contains and controls the horse's performance. This limits the amount of expression. Relinquish control and allow the energy to be channeled or directed. Like water flowing through a pipe, its energy is directed to the place of intention. The water is not out of control but is gently guided. This is "effortless effort."

"Effortless effort" allows more control. The rider synchronizes with the rhythm of the horse and channels the energy to utilize and direct the performance instead of controlling and blocking the expression. The natural rhythm of the horse is like a soft guiding light inviting you to follow. You follow the light allowing it to guide the performance yet at the same time you connect with "inner rhythm" *(Part Four, Spirit)* and remain constant or still in your actions. The energy generated sustains the rider and the performance becomes effortless. The rider benefits by increased stamina and clarity of mind because the energy is focused and concentrated instead of dispersed and erratic. Control of the horse is achieved by following the movement and adapting to each circumstance instead of using brute strength.

"Effortless effort" is a spontaneous action or motion that allows expression directed by intention. It is non-action within an action. For example: Remember the time during the fifth or sixth grade when you so innocently threw a spit ball at the blackboard, not caring where it landed, and not concerned about the consequence? You were simply expressing yourself. This is "effortless effort."

Each time you nonchalantly hit a golf ball, you are exercising effortless effort. Ever notice how, some days, your ride seemed impeccable? Perhaps on that day, you unconsciously did not try to achieve anything in particular and just rode. You rode from instinct, without any effort. A mind state of *mushin* is attained. Effortless effort achieves results. Freedom of expression is cultivated. Don't question what you know. Live what you know by expressing it effortlessly.

· · ·

PART FOUR
SPIRIT

INTRODUCTION

The manifestation of spirit cultivates understanding and insight into the wisdom of nature. The knowledge and experience gained in the process allows for spiritual evolution reconnecting the soul to the source or creator. The act of developing a skill into an art nurtures this process of spiritual evolution by providing the tools needed for individual growth and soul awareness.

Equestrian art is the perfect element, as it offers the necessary tools for self-development. The goal of the rider is to be in perfect harmony with the horse. This can be reached when the rider develops perfect harmony within the three aspects of themselves. The development of the body has physical limitations and is constrained by the mind. The spirit goes beyond that which is tangible. The unification of body, mind and spirit provides the window of opportunity for greater learning and soul evolution.

The greatest gift you can offer humanity is the free expression of your higher self or soul identity. It is the embodiment of the creator and requires a profound understanding and respect for the laws of nature. Mankind cannot evolve without this wisdom.

. . .

INNER RHYTHM

The best way to describe "inner rhythm" is being in "the zone." (*Part Three, No Mind*). It is the rhythm of the soul. It is a strong sense of well-being. Every living thing has an "inner rhythm." When it is in balance, there is harmony. If the balance of "inner rhythm" is jeopardized, there is illness, fatigue, mental confusion or a total breakdown.

Modern lifestyles often conflict with "inner rhythm." Everyone is in a hurry. Look around you; the trees do not rush to grow. Why does a child feel so pressured to hurry up and grow older? It is society's programming. The precious moments of every day are wasted because of hastiness. Society has dictated the rhythm in which to live. It is unconsciously accepted. Rush hour is a good example of this. Hurry to work, hurry home, rush at work, and gulp down your lunch. Where is the fire? What are you trying to achieve that cannot be done in a peaceful, natural rhythm?

Hastiness is how horses are dealt with. Riding time is squeezed into the already full schedule. The horse is quickly tacked and hastily ridden. The horse feels pressure. It must hurry to please the rider. The horse gets upset, his "inner rhythm" is disturbed, and the ride falls apart.

A rider who lacks connectivity with his personal "inner rhythm" transfers this to the horse. The horse translates this as having to put up with an insecure rider. This is demonstrated on a deeper level of sympathetic vibration. *(Part Two, Body Awareness)*. For instance, a horse running on the forehand in a quick rhythm and being evasive to the aids of the rider demonstrates a lack of "inner rhythm". The energy is driven down instead of up and forward. *(Part Two, Illustration C)*. The horse takes full advantage of a rider who has displaced "inner rhythm."

The horse learns that running on the forehand is acceptable. If the rider cannot recognize this loss of rhythm, the horse continues to assume that the fast rhythm is correct. The rider needs to reconnect with personal "inner rhythm" in order to rectify the situation. Once the rider can do this, it is easier to correct and recognize the evasions of the horse. The rider thinks, "Gee, no wonder I was having so much trouble maintaining leg contact and getting the horse on the bit." Connectivity with the horse is reestablished. Suddenly, the horse is happy to oblige because he is comfortable when ridden in his natural rhythm.

Regaining personal "inner rhythm" is easy. One simple way is to hold an infant. Ever notice how you and the baby connect? Somehow, subconsciously, you begin to rock the baby. This is "inner rhythm." If you watch others as they hold the infant, everyone seems to pick up the same rhythm. It is universal.

Watch a well-ridden horse trot effortlessly within the rhythm of its stride. Different breeds have different length of stride, speed, suspension, impulsion, etc., but the "inner rhythm" remains constant. A rider disconnected from "inner rhythm" looks like a crash-test dummy, and the horse appears to be running in the opposite direction of the rider. The energy is dispersed. (*Part Two, Illustration C and D*). It needs to be unified.

How do you regain "inner rhythm" in riding? Practice. Ride many horses with a qualified trainer and develop your feel instinct. Look for a trainer who has the qualities you would like to have, especially "inner rhythm." Practice until "inner rhythm" is ingrained as a habit acquired by feel. If practiced consistently, "inner rhythm" becomes stable and recognizable. This is recorded in the "feel" library as an impulse or vibration.

With a certain degree of refinement or recognition of "inner rhythm", the impulse becomes a natural instinct. All that is needed to connect with "inner rhythm" is a vision of the goal. It is an active response to a thought. A simple thought or vision of the goal, such as the correct carriage of a horse ridden within its natural rhythm creates the goal. The rider's body is conditioned to respond and seeks the right feel by applying the correct aids while making necessary adjustments to remain in balance with the horse. Feel connects personal "inner rhythm" with that of your horse allowing expression in each stride.

A properly trained rider does not think how to ride a half-pass; instead, he expects to ride it by feel. The half-pass is thought of in its entirety. The thought is transferred to the body, which complies by applying the proper aids. The horse executes the movement. There is no doubt, only transformation. A rider who lacks "inner rhythm" sends contradictory messages to the horse. The horse is pushed to perform, but at the same time, is told to relax and remain supple.

There is fast food, fast driving, and fast riding. Hurry up to accomplish the goal. Society sets the pace. You live it. With the mind in a state of haste, it is impossible to feel, see and connect with the environment. It is difficult to hurry up and relax simultaneously. Hurrying creates tension of the body and mind, preventing the life force from nourishing the soul. Relaxation releases tension of body, mind and spirit, allowing the movement of the life force to flow through the individual.

For the horse, this concept of hastiness does not exist. To force a horse to hurry up and relax will create a tense and nervous mount. The rider is already defeated. The horse reacts and is reprimanded. This punishment is unjustified. The rider needs to step out of society's rhythm and maintain personal "inner rhythm." Pause for a moment and breathe. Reconnect with the life force that surrounds and supports us. The results are a calm, quiet body, mind, and spirit. Stillness within is the stabilizing factor. The horse responds sympathetically.

A busy mind creates mental confusion and disorderly thinking preventing the rider from synchronizing with "inner rhythm". This can mean skipping one important phase of the training session: the warm-up. This phase not only prepares the horse but the rider as well. The warm-up preps the rider physically, mentally and emotionally inducing relaxation of the body, mind and spirit. The results are shown in the horse as the rider synchronizes his "inner rhythm" with that of the horse.

"Inner rhythm" occurs by focusing the power of the mind. A focused mind encourages letting go by utilizing the function of both hemispheres of the brain. Focused intention moves and directs *Ki (Part Four, Life Force)* like water flows downstream and reconnects the individual with "inner rhythm."

Take a walk in the forest and restore your personal "inner rhythm." Enter the forest by offering your thoughts, opinions and uncertainties to the trees. Empty your mind and trust in the forest around you. A tree holds the wisdom of nature. They possess "inner rhythm." The roots reach deep into the ground and the limbs rise up toward the sky while receiving nourishment from the elements of the earth. Stand as a tree. Plant your feet firmly into the earth while reaching upward with your arms. Face your heart toward the sun and receive your nourishment. Look around, the tree and the forest appear lifeless yet they are filled with life. There is a field of vibrating energy that surrounds you, the tree, the forest and the earth. If you let go and allow connectivity and synchronization with this vibrating energy, you will rock in the rhythm of nature, just as you did by rocking the infant. This is inner rhythm, a peaceful, moving energy field or life force that connects all living things.

As you leave the forest, take the rhythm with you. Do not jump in your car and rush off. Head in your direction, but do it within your rhythm. This does not mean at your own pace. There is a difference. In nature's rhythm, there is a sense of inner peace that allows an individual to function within the rhythm of society, without being affected by it.

Sitting in a traffic jam can be a lesson in how to maintain "inner rhythm." Losing your temper does not affect the traffic jam but it will dictate your emotional state. Stay in the present moment and "inner rhythm" will remain constant.

Riding your horse with a busy mind prevents connectivity with your mount. Instead train your mind to be one hundred percent present and certain about the goal. The present moment is where you find "inner rhythm" and can enter into a state of mushin.

A horse is always in the present moment, content with what he is doing and who he is. They live in harmony with nature. If we can recognize and connect with inner rhythm, we begin to speak the language of nature and therefore that of the horse. Improved communication and fewer confrontations are the result.

"Inner rhythm" is not something that is seen externally, as you would see a horse or tree. It goes beyond the physical elements that comprise life. What are seen are the results of "inner rhythm"— connectivity and synchronization.

Reestablishing "inner rhythm" is a natural progression that develops balanced riding and increased spiritual awareness. How you walk, sit and stand lead to the details of body alignment. This builds self-carriage and balance. After physical development and understanding, the mind is brought into action, cultivating the right atmosphere for spiritual evolution. Riding provides us the golden opportunity to regain personal "inner rhythm" by providing all the essential ingredients.

. . .

LIFE FORCE

Life force, also known as *Ki* ("key"), *Ch'i* ("Chee"), and *Shakti* in Japanese, Chinese, and Hindu systems is universal and translates to "energy" or "vital essence." It guides and directs the growth and life cycle of living things and the basic structure of non-living things. *Ki* is the fundamental energy that sustains life.

This infinite power is the unifying force within us, around us, between others, nature, the earth and the universe. The energy travels on a vibration of high or low frequency that oscillates according to the emotional and spiritual well-being of the individual, as well as a myriad of environmental factors. It is circulated throughout the body in a series of tentacle-like channels, called *nadis* in Hindu and Buddhist systems. In the Chinese healing system, these channels are referred to as acupuncture meridians. The meridians join together in a scheme of plexus, or centers, located along the spine. The union of the centers is called chakras. The nervous system is embedded along the meridians as well. Present in the centers and meridians are the subconscious and unconscious programs of the brain. It is the experience of energy felt in the chakras that brings on different states of emotion. The energy that flows through these centers determines your state of mind, behavior, and general well-being.

Focused intention achieves stimulation and activation of the chakra centers. A simple, concentrated thought directs the current to your place of intention. *(Illustration G)*. A slight tingling or warmth may be noticed as the energy moves through the center to complete the circuit. Negative influences, actions, and thoughts create resistance in the circuit. This interrupts the circulation of the life force or *Ki*. This is similar to a water pipe that gets clogged at a bend. The water slows down at the blockage point. Seepage makes its way through and picks up the debris along the way. The results are reflected in a healthy body and mind, or one inflicted with physical symptoms and ailments, eventually leading to deterioration of the body, mind and spirit. An individual does not create the circuit but determines whether the circuit will be complete and vibrant, or weak and broken. The manner in which the energy vibrates is determined by the degree of evolution in consciousness of that individual.

The average person cannot see, hear or smell *Ki*, so it is easily tossed aside as being nonexistent. Its relevance to life is too profound for the common mind to doubt. Doubt seeks to prove things on a scientific level. This prevents the heart from feeling and recognizing that which is real.

Daily, *Ki* is unconsciously directed and exchanged. A casual handshake exchanges *Ki*. Sometimes, the handshake feels sincere and warm, while other times, it is cold and distrusting. *Ki* is unconsciously directed by the innermost thoughts and intentions of the individual. *(Illustration G)*. A warm thought of a loved one can bring them knocking at your door or ringing your phone. The quality of your thoughts determines the outcome or experience by determining the direction and intention of *Ki*.

A rider can create a negative situation with his horse by his unconscious intentions of fear and doubt or aggressiveness and intimidation. The horse responds to the negative intentions as well as to external stimuli. Negative intention receives negative reactions. Positive intentions receive positive reactions.

An individual who dislikes horses or, perhaps, is afraid of them, directs this fear on a subconscious level to the horse. The horse interprets the intention and begins to react by displaying anxious or nervous behavior. A horse will not cooperate with an individual who presents an aversion. This is the natural response of all living things.

Similarly, an individual is uncomfortable around someone they don't trust. Tightness in the solar plexus region or heart center arises and creates a feeling of uneasiness. *Ki* is responsible for these sensations. Honest intention produces strong communication between horse and rider, and between person to person.

Intention maintains uninterrupted movement of *Ki,* recycling from horse to rider and rider to horse. Intention is directed and applied by a simple thought. *(Illustration G).* The thought is received and the body responds, provided the mind is void of uncertainty. Doubt inhibits and restricts the cycle. Once the cycle is restricted, it becomes a disadvantage to the rider by making it more difficult to feel body alignment and the intentions of the horse. Congested *Ki* creates tension. Tension is what you don't want when riding a horse. Inner rhythm and synchronization are lost. Apply a clear intention that assists and encourages the horse to respond appropriately and allows the horse to perform within its level of ability. The inner rhythm of the rider to the horse is synchronized by the flow of *Ki.*

. . .

Graphic representation of how thought forms driven by intention form the catalyst for materialization

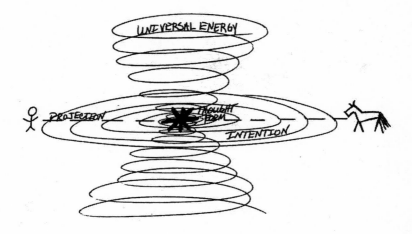

Illustration G

Thought form or mental imagery is directed from the individual or rider, generating an energy vortex by the force of intention. This acts as a catalyst, directing it to the place or object of intention. This energy cannot take a solid shape at this point, or it is limited in its own ability to transform, concentrate or disperse. When it reaches the place of intention or the horse, it is immediately received and transmuted back around in a continuous cycle, until the intention becomes limited by the mind and breaks the circuit.

• • •

Directing *Ki* is essential to the art of equitation. It can mean the difference between harmony and elegance, or rough and crude. A rider who synchronizes personal "inner rhythm" with that of the horse has less difficulty in directing and understanding *Ki*.

Ki is the carrying energy of the horse and rider. *(Illustration E)*. *Ki* always seeks balance. It effortlessly maintains harmony of the rider and his mount. *Ki* aligns the rider to the horse. Alignment is balance. Balance is freedom. Freedom allows motion. Motion creates energy. Energy is *Ki*. *Ki* synchronizes horse and rider, developing into true equestrian art.

. . .

BREATH

The health of your entire being is affected by the functioning of your breath. Thoughts and emotions affect your respiration and heartbeat. A classic example is the effects of stress on the heart, the breathing rate, and the digestive system. Symptoms such as shortness of breath, rapid heartbeat, indigestion and excessive sweating are a few of the damaging effects of stress. These symptoms inhibit your ability to absorb and utilize external *Ki*. Simply put, it becomes difficult to breathe naturally.

Natural breathing is centered in the *hara* (Japanese) or *Tan Tien* (Chinese), located two fingers below the navel, or approximately three cm (1.25 in.). It is in line with the suspension point at the top of your head. Picture a wooden puppet. When the string attached through the center of the puppet is pulled, the puppet's wooden parts stack on top of one another. They fall into alignment. This is similar to your spine and the stacking of your vertebrae. This analogy is commonly used among riding instructors, as correct posture and alignment is described to the rider. *(Illustration H)*

When the inner suspension points are out of alignment, correct position on the horse is impossible. Collected work involves a higher degree of alignment of the suspension points. Alignment enables the rider to suspend in cadence with the suspension of the horse's stride. Elevation of the horse is then effortless.

Suspension offers freedom of movement through the topline of the horse and expansion of the rib cage, promoting deep breathing for the horse and rider.

SUSPENSION POINTS

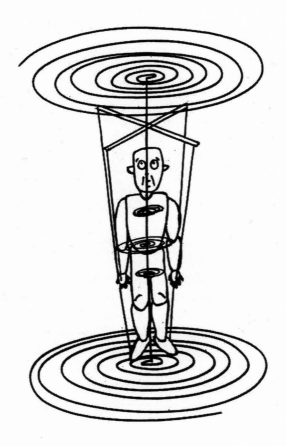

Illustration H

The top of the head, or the crown chakra, aligns with the base of the spine, or root chakra. The center of gravity, or *hara,* connects with these two suspension points to provide stability. Heaven and Earth's energy flows in a direct current through these channels and interlinks the other chakra centers. If these centers are off balance, the flow of internal and external *ki* is interrupted and redirected. The result is discomfort, ill health or a lack of balance.

Breathing from the *hara* refocuses the energy in the center of the body and aligns the inner suspension points. This manner of breathing is different from the shallow, quick breathing of the chest. Abdominal breathing is deep and powerful.

A rider with a well-developed *hara* breathes deeply and is well-balanced. The muscles of the abdomen are flexible and the diaphragm has maximum freedom. The upper body is firmly supported by the lower body in what is termed "grounded," or a "deep seat." To a rider, a deep seat insures balance. A rider experiences sitting "into" the saddle, as opposed to on top of it *(Part Two, Body Awareness)*. The legs drape around the rib cage of the horse in a relaxed but stable position, instead of gripping with the knee and rising up. A deep seat promotes a longer leg, which, in turn, provides greater connectivity with the horse.

Breathing from the *hara* is breathing naturally, allowing *Ki* to circulate throughout your entire being. Deep *hara* breathing requires a conscious effort to activate it. A rider initiating the aids from the *hara* circulates *Ki* from the seat, to the leg, to the horse, and to the hands, and back again for regeneration. *(See illustration D)*.

It is important to note that it is regenerated and rejuvenated. The hands and wrists do not lock and pull on the reins. This is often misunderstood. Every gait of the horse, including backing and the halt, is a forward motion. It is not a stopping action; instead, the hands act as guides to collect, direct or redirect the forward movement.

Proper riding develops the vitality of the *hara*. This is accomplished through balance, alignment, stamina and breathing. As the rider releases tension, the center of gravity is automatically lowered developing a deeper seat. This is a breath of release and allowance. Breathe a good sigh of relief and improve your balance.

A strong, well-developed *hara* is an essential ingredient for balanced riding. The development of the *hara* determines the amount of rider synchronization with the horse. A strong *hara* is able to maintain centeredness amidst chaos, meaning the rider remains composed and does not become unseated in adverse situations. The aids are simply applied, with more intention within a level of composure. Nervousness and excitability in the horse are prevented. The intention is felt by the horse and in most cases, the horse complies. To maintain composure during periods of disobedience, the rider must breathe.

The breath of your horse is equally influential. Listen to the breath of your horse. It indicates his acceptance or disapproval of your aids. Take note that when he is tense or disobedient, the breath is short and quick. Upon relaxation and acceptance of the aids, he immediately responds with a large, deep exhale. Listening to the breath of the horse provides the rider connectivity to the mind of the horse.

Are you out of breath after an attempt at your first leg yield? What about your horse? Unless you are riding a horse that is a conditioned athlete or one that is ridden more than you ride, you can be sure he is, too. Use the breath as a guide when to allow a moment of rest. Give your horse a loose rein and allow him to stretch his neck to the ground and inhale some rejuvenating air.

Connecting your breath with that of your horse completes the circuit of *Ki*. This is done on a subtle level of synchronicity, where the "inner rhythms" of horse and rider meet. Riders tend to hold their breath. By doing this, the circuit is broken, tension arises and the cycle begins again. Before reprimanding your mount, check your breath and reconnect your *hara*. Difficulties can easily be resolved by deep breathing.

In many circumstances, holding of the breath creates a reaction in the horse as well. He responds by exhibiting signs of disapproval and disobedience. *(Sympathetic Vibration)*. This can evolve into a dangerous situation if not dealt with properly and expediently. If in doubt, bring the horse to a walk immediately, and breathe deeply. Keep breathing until the horse relaxes. This indicates a release. Reconnect your "inner rhythm" and begin again.

Check that your aids are precise and clear, your position is balanced, and your timing of the aids is synchronized with the stride of horse. There can be numerous reasons for the disruption of energy between the horse and rider. If all else fails, reflect upon your breath and inner feelings.

The rider with a weak *hara* is easily thrown off balance by tension and emotional energy. The energy rises and the center of gravity becomes unstable. Regain your center of gravity by breathing, and give yourself credit when you do. Always maintain control of emotional energy. It determines the strength of the *hara* and the potential of your horse.

Breathing plays a vital role in the integration of body, mind and spirit. It is said that the breath is the key to self-realization. The breath preserves physical and mental balance while producing inner strength and vitality. It is the expression of life.

In conclusion, the strength of the *hara* determines the amount of synchronicity between the horse and rider. It is an essential element that cannot be overlooked. Balance is controlled by the *hara,* and the breath controls synchronicity. Without synchronicity, the rider merely sits on top of the horse while his body bounces around uncontrollably and his mind wanders carelessly, waiting for an accident.

• • •

LOVE

To become one with the object of your intention is an expression of love. The goal of the rider is to ride in harmony and oneness with their mount. This is accomplished through devotion and dedication to the art of equitation and to the horse. When all actions are initiated from the heart unconditionally, harmonious relationships are the result. Any art motivated by love transforms into an expression of love.

All animals express unconditional love to us and to other animals as well. This can be demonstrated through body language such as two horses entwined at the neck and nuzzling the withers of one another. The expression of love may differ due to species and habits but the message is the same. A dog may wag its tail and offer obedience as an expression of love, while a cat will purr in contentment. A horse offers love by his soft nickers and submissive eye. His eagerness to greet you at the gate is an expression of love. A horse shows admiration and respect for an individual he trusts. This is a reflection of love.

Emotional and physical challenges are easier when love is the motivational tool. For the rider, difficulties are overcome in a moment of synchronicity. The horse rewards this action with love by expression in his movement and transfers this to the rider. Immediately, there is a sense of gratification and the hard work is forgotten. If the rider is committed and loves what he is doing, the horse will be happy and willing to work. Without love, the horse becomes unresponsive to the world around them and the work is dull and arduous. It is sympathetic.

Self-expression and love are demonstrated in the body carriage and alignment of an individual. For instance, forward-sloping, sagging shoulders with a collapsed chest reveals an area of protection around the heart and solar plexus region. *(Part Two, Body Alignment).* This is an emotional barrier representing hurt. Riding offers an opportunity to overcome this limitation by aligning the posture and building strength of character, thus assisting in the release of emotional energy.

The way this works is as follows: As the rider improves their body position on the horse, the shoulders open, allowing freedom in the chest cavity. This expands the lung capacity. The rider can breathe properly. The breath moves the life force through the chakra centers, thus, the emotional energy detaches. The results are seen as a more relaxed gait and an impression of freedom in the horse. Postural alignment, balance, and strength of character determine success or failure. Love of the horse is the catalyst.

Love builds strength of character and bonds man with the animal kingdom. It touches the soul of all living things and by doing so, nurtures physical, mental and spiritual healing on an individual level as well as universally. Love is the language of the universe. It has the power to create life and unite life. Unity is infinite oneness with the Creator. Love is a magnetic force that draws and binds every one of us from a level of compassion. When you learn to forgive, you learn to love. Love is the law of nature and the mind of the universe. Let love into your life.

. . .

PASSION

Webster's Dictionary defines passion as "a powerful feeling." Passion provides the drive and motivation in the pursuit of equestrian art. It is generated by love. Love for the horse ignites passion and brings joy into your life. Joy provides fulfillment. Now, there is a purpose. The purpose is joy. Passion fuels it and an individual contributes to society by becoming that purpose.

To delve into employment because of salary benefits, but disliking the work is not the path to find joy. Passion is lost. Purpose is denied. Dignity and grace are abandoned. Love dies. Without purpose, there is no passion. Existence becomes mundane.

It takes courage to possess passion. It means standing up for yourself and what you believe in. There may be ridicule when you decide to quit your corporate job and pursue what is in your heart. Overcome the fear of rejection and you will find passion. It lies dormant in the hearts of all mankind. Awaken it in yours. Experience the change that occurs.

Love for horses is addictive. This addiction generates a passion for knowledge. The saying, "It's in my blood" indicates a deep passion. Horse people generally have passion. They have to. Owning horses requires immense obligation. To not have passion would be like one of the walking dead. Loving the smell and presence of horses is a passion only those who have lived it know.

Rediscover passion by seeking that which brings you joy. Passion lies there. Experience it by living it. The reward is harmony with your horse and love in your life.

. . .

JOY

Love and passion brings an individual to the discovery of joy. Where there is harmony, there is joy. It is a deep contentment and knowingness within yourself and the surrounding environment.

Joy resolves issues in life. Clarity is gained. There are no issues. There is no longer anything missing because of fullness, which is really emptiness. Experience the fullness or joy and discover peace in your heart.

Joy dissolves stress. Bringing joy into your life should become second nature. You simply are all that you are. Imperfections dissipate, self-expression emanates. Others around you benefit. It is contagious.

The horse is a beneficiary of your fulfillment. The horse enjoys the freedom and understanding that it now receives. Joy allows you to step into the mind of the horse. This happens by synchronizing with the horse, the final goal.

There is great satisfaction, knowing that all challenges lead to guaranteed fulfillment, provided the laws of nature are abided by. In your struggle for perfection, do not forget that perfection already exists. This is where joy lives.

. . .

SATORI

A sudden flash of enlightenment is *satori*. This can be described as a state of intuitive alignment or illumination. Words such as unity, bliss or oneness all describe this state of being. There a many levels and lengths to the experience of *satori*. This is determined by the individual responsiveness to the satori. To reach total enlightenment, the body and mind are in absolute alignment with the light of spirit and a new perspective on life is acquired.

More simply put, *satori* is the place where black and white merge. There is no longer separation of the body, mind and spirit. Instead, the entire being immerses with the task of daily living. Simplicity and clarity replaces the limitations of the mind, allowing thoughts and actions to originate from a place of pure intention.

The goal of the rider is oneness with the horse. This is accomplished by diligent practice to develop skill and internal and external harmony. A moveable and tranquil body and mind are the results. *Satori* offers expansion to the rider as awareness increases and elevates. (*Zanchin, Part One, Communication*).

A solid foundation in any art nurtures *satori*. Developing good posture and alignment, a positive outlook, strength of mind, deep breathing, and proper nourishment are factors in building a foundation that supports natural law. This "right way" encourages harmony individually as well as universally and initiates soul realization or *bussho*, a place of knowingness. Equestrian art is the perfect breeding ground for discovering your true potential. It provides the rider with the opportunity to develop a greater understanding of natural law, thereby sustaining the "right way" of life.

Satori or oneness supports this "right way" by offering discovery of the whole experience of existence thus incorporating peace, harmony and love into daily life. Actions are initiated from the heart offering freedom from the limitations of the mind. This brings an individual closer to the wisdom of *bussho*. Satori must be experienced to awaken to your true potential otherwise the reflection of the soul is cloudy and dull. Disciplined efforts of the individual allow clarity of the mind and an occasional taste of *satori*. Like the honeybee that cannot resist the sweet nectar of a flower, once *satori* is experienced, it ignites a passion for pursuing the path of enlightenment.

The art of equitation encourages this path of enlightenment by providing the essential elements needed to achieve this state of being. Training a horse requires focused effort. Intensity of focus, concentration, and discipline determine the degree of oneness with the horse. For the rider, this means the degree to which they have aligned the body, mind and spirit. Oneness with the horse brings joy and connectivity to the surrounding environment. In this realm, everything is accomplished in a state of joy and experienced from the heart.

It is easy to gain an intellectual grasp of *satori*. One cannot know it without experiencing it. To experience *satori*, one must purify the mind and expand the heart. *Satori* initiates individual understanding of life and a profound truth of nature that leads to higher wisdom or soul-realization.

. . .

CONCLUSION

To be the master of any art, first, become the master of yourself; then, you will understand the pureness of the art. It does not matter what discipline you choose as your tool to spiritual unity. What matters is that you have chosen to walk the path of spiritual unity. Recognizing this is the necessary foundation that cultivates higher wisdom and understanding.

The aim is to develop our full potential. This potential is expressed according to natural law. Devotion to equestrian art develops the rider's potential and gives active proof of your faith in nature. Reverence for the Creator guides the individual to manifest divine potential.

Every animal has something to teach humanity. Each has certain qualities that reflect back to humans a most desired quality of themselves. The rabbit is quick and instinctive, with ears that never miss a sound; the eagle has eyes to see even the smallest detail; the mountain lion has the courage of ten men, he is fearless; the ground hog loves to remain hidden in darkness, only to be seen if he chooses to; and the horse is swift and elegant with his constant movement. He's the wild yet tamed spirit in all of us. All of them represent free existence. They are what they are. They remain unchanged in basic character strengths.

There are five essential elements required to develop and walk the path of spiritual unity. All promote world harmony and require an active role from you, the initiator. The first of these elements is the way of fearlessness, the ability to conquer one's innermost conflicts. One must first recognize and then face these issues. This heals the body, mind and spirit. The cultivation of fearlessness develops compassion, understanding, and respect. There must be love and utmost reverence toward whatever understanding one seeks. One must dissolve all doubts and walk in absolute fearlessness. *Mountain lion*

Second is the way of vision. One must develop insight and understand all things, such as the mountains, the sky, the ocean, and of course, the horse. Life is filled with peace and harmony when one sees with the heart as well as the mind. The heart will understand things the mind cannot grasp. Learn to see with the whole body, mind and spirit. *Eagle.*

Third is the way of listening. Listen to all things without discretion. Learn to listen to the wisdom of the wind and the earth; it encompasses the rhythm of nature. Learn to hear the sounds of silence. They are the embodiment of the Creator. All knowledge can be heard by one who listens. *Rabbit.*

Fourth is the path of silent shadows. Walk in the shadows of humbleness. Nurture security in silence. Everything in the light, as well as the darkness, can be seen, felt, and known. One who walks the path of silent shadows proclaims little and takes little credit for self. Often, it is not the priest who is the wise one, but the gardener who walks in silence, unnoticed. This one is worth looking into. *Ground Hog.*

The last is the way of existence. One must become the trees, the sky, and the stars. There must be an unshakable, but not frozen, attitude amongst constant change. One must feel their existence as part of the Creator. If it is understood and lived, one cannot fail. Failure comes from within the individual. It is not an external influence. To live in harmony with all that is becomes the "right way." Compassion and understanding replace discord. All things function from a level of harmony within nature. Higher wisdom offers freedom. Freedom offers movement. *Horse*

When all five qualities come together in absolute alignment, an individual radiates with the infinite wealth, power, and wisdom of the universe. Spirituality is simplicity.

Every individual who climbs halfway up the mountain increases world peace. Those who sit at the bottom and procrastinate will never reach the top. Instead, they become burdens at the foot of the mountain, transforming into obstacles for others to either climb over or assist. Share what insight you have to help them take the first step to climb the mountain. Assist by teaching them to help themselves by taking individual responsibility. This builds a world of peace, harmony and love.

. . .

GLOSSARY

Automatic
Acuity

Autonomically receiving and translating information through the right hemisphere of the brain; automatic keenness of perception

Bussho

A place of knowingness or state of being referred to as Buddha-nature; rooted in the structure of living cells, represents our true potential.

Chakra

Sanskrit for "centers". The point at which the *nadis* (Indian) or energy meridians of the body collide to produce an explosive whirlpool of energy allowing entrance and exit of internal and external *Ki*. Psychic senseorgans; places where the sensation of energy is concentrated in any human experience. Eastern physiology recognizes seven major chakra centers located in the body.

Dozen

Movement performed with heightened responsiveness; moving meditation.

Effortless Effort

Spontaneous endeavor which allows expression; non-action within an action.

Feel sense

To perceive, become conscious of, and have mental sensations other than by sight, hearing, taste, or smell. An impression often used reflexively and usually followed by a complement; the way a rider learns to ride.

Fixation   A partial arrest of an instinctual or emotional development.

Hara   The lower abdominal center of the nervous system and musculature; the physical and emotional center of gravity. The center responsible for stability and balance. Known as *Uddiyana* in India, *T'an T'ien* in China, and transliterated into Japanese as *Tanden*.

Inner Rhythm   The rhythm of one's spiritual being. The patterned reoccurrence of harmonic movement within the human body.

Ki   Super intelligent, cosmic life energy sometimes referred to as universal energy. Called Prana (India) Ch'i (China).

Nadis   A series of branching channels or meridians running throughout the body carrying an electrical charge that moves energy from point to point in a continuous flow to maintain the life force. The path of the subtle nervous system.

Satori   An experience of enlightenment or awakening: an intuitive alignment which is given by the truth and understanding of human nature. In India, it is known as *Samadhi* or *Nirvana*, and is known by many other names throughout the world.

Synchronicity   The point at which an attempted reconciliation or union, in this context, body, mind and spirit, merges simultaneously to become a state of existence.

Sympathetic Vibration   A relationship between horse and rider in which the condition of one induces a parallel or reciprocal condition in another. This also applies in human relationships.

Zanchin   A dynamic state of readiness that implies instantaneous and appropriate response to a situation or circumstance.

Zen   Buddhism, a Mahayana movement, introduced in China in the 6th century a.d. and in Japan in the 12th century A.D. The emphasis is upon enlightenment of the student by direct intuitive insight and applied to every aspect of human existence.

. . .